BEST *of* AUSTRALIAN POEMS 2025

I0674531

ACKNOWLEDGEMENT
OF COUNTRY

Australian Poetry is based
in Naarm, Melbourne, working
in offices and remotely on both
Wurundjeri Woi Wurrung and
Boon Wurrung lands.
We acknowledge their Elders,
past and present. As a national
poetry body, we also acknowledge
that we work across many lands and
communities, and we extend our
deep respect to all First Peoples, not
just in Australia, but across the globe,
including poets and audiences, and
their enduring connection
to Country.

Best of Australian Poems
SERIES PUBLISHER
Australian Poetry

BEST *of* AUSTRALIAN POEMS 2025

GUEST EDITORS

JILL JONES

&

NAM LE

First published 2025 by
Australian Poetry
www.australianpoetry.org

National Library of Australia
Cataloguing-in-Publication data:
Best of Australian Poems 2025
ISBN: 978-0-9923189-6-3

Publisher: Australian Poetry (Acting Publisher, Martin Dolan) / australianpoetry.org
Guest Editors: Nam Le, Jill Jones
Volume Editor (freelance): Jacinta Le Plastrier
Editorial Associate / Social Media Communications: Jennifer Nguyen
Designer and Typesetter: Chris Edwards
Cover Design: Sophie Gaur
Printer: Lightning Source

Publisher's Note

It is AP's policy as publisher across all our publications to remain independent from the selection of poems and editorial commentary made by our guest editors, whose autonomy and curatorial independence we fiercely respect. First Nations Cultural Protocols are also strictly followed, as directed by AP's First Nations Cultural Protocols Director, Yvette Henry Holt. Separately to this, any use of another person's work by contributors is expected to be acknowledged in notes, and the responsibility for this, along with biographies supplied, remains with the poets. We also respect spelling and grammatical variations of poets. New guest editors are appointed for all publications and the themes of publications are finalised and commissioned 12–18 months ahead of each, as required by funding timelines. AP takes its responsibilities to provide methods of excellence and support, and assiduous editorial production processes extremely seriously with very high, proven skill sets among those who work on our projects; this includes offering our duty of care to guest editors, other editors, all contributors, editorial, design and production associates, readers and audiences, and staff. Poetry is a language for life, a trued and compassionate, also exploratory and experimental, language of essence, which has provided meaning for all communities across millennia.

Support

AP would like to thank all publishers, platforms and other organisations that support the flourishing of Australian poetry. We particularly thank our core funders for supporting this publication, which has been assisted by the Australian Government through Creative Australia, its arts funding and advisory body. We also thank a number of generous, private patrons.

Foreword

First we would like to acknowledge the traditional owners of the unceded lands on which this book was edited and produced, including the lands of the Kaurna, Wurundjeri and Boon Wurrung peoples. A number of poems in this anthology were written by First Nations writers and we pay our respects to the long traditions of song and storytelling that are integral to these sovereign lands.

Best of Australian Poems 2025 is the fifth anthology of Australian Poetry's series that aims to bring together some of the most surprising, most intriguing, most challenging work by Australian poets within a twelve month timeframe, covering July 2024 to June 2025. We intended in our selection to register the resonances both loud and soft, the struggles, the energies of this particular year. We editors come from different places, generations, cultures, and language spaces, and our discussions, contentions, discoveries, and enthusiasms have led, we hope, to making a volume that offers a broad and engaging view of Australian poetry.

In this volume you will find the free and the formal, lineated and prose forms, lyric and experiment, rant and refusal, conceptual and words straight from the heart, archive and in-the-moment, the speaking and the spoken, the private and the performed, manifestoes and partly secret languages, protests and elegies (often in the same poem), satire and tragedy *and* comedy, inventories, shapes and gaps, collaborations and re/quotations, languages other than English, including First Nations languages, very long and very short poems, story and dialogue, poems from new books, sparkling new unpublished (till now) poems, and the less categorisable.

The aboutness of the poems was, as we'd hoped and expected, as wide as poetry, as the life poetry encompasses. There was death and birth, of course, love and sex, body and gender, sickness and health, family and conflict, the weather inside and outside, places and paths, fact, history and archive, future imaginings and endings, the actual challenges of being a writer in these times. There was much intensity (even quietness can be intense, of course), so there were joys, yes, and also critique, sadness and anger, to be expected in the face of the enormous crises of our moment: climate emergency, environmental devastation, extinctions, ongoing violence against First Nations peoples and cultures, the many other violences in word and deed against so many cultures and identities, the theft of words and livelihoods by AI and all its enabling systems.

And, of course, Gaza, where a horror of mass killing, ethnic cleansing, starvation, humiliation and total destruction of the conditions of life of an entire population is taking place in front of the world's eyes, while world leaders and diplomats argue about legalities, still support the genocide, or plan so-called 'peace initiatives'. As Hasib Hourani writes in 'i see a photo of a great heron ...':

> it's not enough
> it won't do
> we can't only choke
> back the state that chokes us when
>   the state that chokes us
> is being breathed alive
>   by bigger empires

We read, then read again, compiled our own long lists. On Whatsapp and Google Docs and Zoom, over thousands of words and hundreds of minutes we discussed, argued, agreed, and agreed to disagree with each other and ourselves. We changed our minds and each other's, and sometimes changed them back again. We took as open a definition of 'Australian poetry' as we could or were granted. In fact, we pushed that pretty far.

To give a sense of this to and fro and the process of making a volume such as this, we offer this Q&A.

∗

NL: Jill! Here we are, on the other side. I'd be keen to hear your thoughts: on the poems, on the poems as gestalt, on process, on the rules and roles of the thing. How it accorded or not with your expectations. What your expectations were. What was hard, or surprising, or noteworthy for you.

For me—yikes, yes, first off, it was a *lot* of reading. I guess I'm showing my out-of-touchness here but I didn't expect there to be quite so many people writing poetry, nor so many places publishing them. And I'm sure we didn't cover the whole spread. I think 'rude health' was the term you used. What did you mean by this? What was your experience of all this?

JJ: I'll attempt just some of this. Like you, I didn't expect so much material. We read thousands of poems. Poems sent in through the Australian Poetry call out, and poems in so many books and chapbooks, in journals including international ones, both print-based and online, in zines, on social media, poems from performances, and from personal sources. And you're right, I suspect there were things we missed, didn't or couldn't unearth even so. Time, access, all those things came into play. It's a big country. I think it's healthy that there's a lot of regionally based publications and those weren't necessarily publishing writing that was 'regional' in an obvious home town kind of way, but were publishing poets who were taking on all kinds of subjects.

As for what is hard, one of the hardest is the expectation that can accrue around a certain poet, a 'name' in some cases, or simply someone whose work I have known for a long time. I was happy to be surprised by poets doing what I didn't expect. And certainly writers I knew little or nothing about are doing some great things with language, pushing it around, a lot. I was looking for some kind of field of energy in the poem, a pitch of feeling or presence, or a continual torquing of form and subjectivity, the poem as more than its parts.

Another thing I found hard was trying to grab one poem from a whole book in some cases. The kind of book that read like one long piece. It felt that separating the poem from the surrounding ones diminished it. We managed to extract some work that was intimately connected within the whole book in a few cases but that was difficult, wasn't it?

I have been wondering about your expectations, given a lot of the poets and the poetry scenes they are part of might have felt unfamiliar to you. Was there anything that surprised you, either in the poetics or the themes?

NL: Hmmm, it feels tricky talking about poetics and themes because, obviously, there are elements of chance, elements of confirmation bias that come into play—and it's irresistible to look for patterns and then just like *pile* meaning onto them (e.g. so much plant life, so many swimming pools ... let now the reasons unravel themselves ...).

What did I expect? A gamut, I guess, of forms, styles and concerns. And that we got. But as for how this variety slotted into local schools or scenes—you're right, I was very glad to have you alongside. If I was surprised by anything, it was perhaps by how well distributed the variety seemed to be. Take a poem from any one place, press, or periodical; you could imagine it coming from most other places, presses, or periodicals without too much of a squint. (Like your regional but not provincial poets.) Or maybe it's not surprising at all: people—and poetics—move around. Am I off here? Let me know if I'm smoothing out the lumps.

JJ: I agree that there was an abundance of style, theme, form from all over the country. You could, of course, feel the places of the big city poets at times, at least I could imagine some of the streets and places they gestured towards. I'm speaking as a city girl, here. Of course, it was obvious when they named places. Or I could get some of the ways certain poems appeared to feel their way around the styles and forms, indeed obsessions, of certain what you could call 'schools' (a term I don't think is terribly useful, it's too limiting and has a whiff of the doctrinaire).

There *are* lumps of course but there's a breadth that place or poetics doesn't always account for. There is nothing monolithic about Australian poetry. This should go without saying but it needs to be remembered alongside the problems raised by the word 'best'. Many of the poets in this book would align themselves, or be aligned by readers and critics with various kinds of approaches, movements, tendencies, poetics, some of which may even have a declared or undeclared manifesto of sorts, or who are deliberately oppositional. Others would actively refuse or simply not fit established or even the less defined categories or stances. Not all poets are part of a group with some kind of common aesthetic. They don't hang around reading scenes, and their influences and obsessions will move in ways harder to pin down.

NL: Yeah, nah, I agree. I'd go even further. This whole exercise—i.e. anthologising, i.e. curation—is beholden to an ethos of representation that does my head in. Like, how, exactly, is a poem 'representative' of a book or body of work, let alone any larger clumping? To me, a poem is a thing-in-itself, a singular arrangement of words, or it is nothing. To say that it represents anything bigger is synecdochal smudging. Shorthand. And shorthand has its uses, but in (I would argue) different registers than the register of the poem.

Yet here we are, forced to flap about in these registers. Navigating notions of representation and proportion, abstracting poems into aesthetic and political and cultural and regional expressions. Bottling something vast and various (Australian poetry) in a closed book in a way that somehow contains something of this vastness and variousness. Your point about poetic schools puts me in mind of that old joke about hipsters: weird how everyone else is obviously one but not me … Weird how other poets are so easily pegged to this or that school, whereas me—I contain multitudes!

JJ: Haha! Containing multitudes, at least those of Australian poetry, the complexities and divergences. You can't, obviously no-one can, but we did make this gesture. And hopefully the very mix of poems and poetics here encourages a reader to think/read into forms of variousness they may not have come across before.

NL: And what of pleasure? The pleasure of a poem in play with our subjectivities? The pleasure of questioning and breaking out of our patterns of enjoyment? What role does pleasure play in the current of these 'higher order' considerations?

JJ: Ah, pleasure! It can almost seem like a no-no, as if poetry has to make statements about 'the important things' if we are to take it seriously. Pleasure is important, or why bother. And it has its pains, even if that sounds like a cliché. Pleasure is a freedom to, as you say, break patterns and see things anew in ways we want to keep going with.

Of not treading the well-trodden. We all get pleasure in our own ways. And pleasure, real pleasure, is something that political regimes and cultural establishments, and the purveyors of corporate drabness and conformity, indeed the increasingly utilitarian education sector, don't like. Of course, it's important, even as, or because of the way poems confront the world, its languages, its grammars, the ways we engage with each and every word, the sounds of them, the look of them, the feel of them in our mouths, on our tongues, in our heads. I think of those lines from Dženana Vucic's poem 'Because a wind blazes...': 'What else can we do / with all this anger?'

NL: It's telling, isn't it, how it feels impossible right now to think or talk about anything hyper-personal (like pleasure) without implicating it in broader politics. This is a moment of threat—from rising fascism, from liberal hypocrisy—the two are not unrelated—from neoliberal complicity and corporate and media capture, from xenophobia, from racist and sexist regression, from control of speech and thought. As we write this, the literary journal *Meanjin* has been shuttered on 'purely financial grounds'. Of course pleasure—aka a subjective state that need not explain itself—is under attack.

Speaking of outward entanglement, you said it best, I think, when you spoke of what accrues around a poet. We went through a fair bit of argy-bargy with interpretive admin, didn't we, about every rung of our mandate: what 'best' meant, or 'of', or 'Australian' or 'poem' (even '2025'—which meant the financial year of (?!)—wasn't without complication)—all of the litigations that vent their way through these kinds of anthology intros, which is why I appreciated how you cut to the quick. What accrues around a poet. Or a poem. Expectation, as you say, which enlivens the question: Of what? Of name and reputation, yes, which then enlivens the question of context—in time, in tradition, in discourse, in critical ecology, in a body of work, in a collection or journal or anthology, in conversation? In a way, our task—of looking, one by one, at the thing (i.e. the poem) itself—was inseparable from— secondary to?—the task of orchestrating all the peripheral accruals around the things. Does that make sense to you?

JJ: Orchestration is a good term for this. I did wonder about why these 'best of' anthologies weren't edited by just one person, as in 'let's see what x or y thinks about this year of poetry, in some quite specific take'. But having actually done it, I feel that involving two people to bounce the poems around adds something to the process. It lets you, forces you in some cases, to really read and often re-read a poem, to see what the other editor sees, positively or otherwise. None of us are neutral, obviously, and my choice isn't always yours, or mine next week, or what I might feel in three months' time. And we don't have to, and didn't always, agree with each other or even our own selves at various stages. I was so glad you were there to keep me focused and aware of my own perspectives, not to negate them, but negotiate them.

But back to pleasure for a moment, the closing down of *Meanjin* certainly indicates that universities, in this kind of instance but even more widely than this, are no longer fully supportive of the arts, humanities or creative research, unless it suits their corporate agendas or Government labour market requirements. Of course, other forces are also operating to close down creative and critical questioning and dissent across the board. Yes, I am refusing to separate pleasure and politics at this point!

NL: So depressing, the capitulation of universities right when the need for them to be and do what they were created to be and do is greatest. But on a brighter note: right back at you!—I can't think of a better person to have bounced with. And I want to underline the point you just made: that this anthology is a snapshot of a dynamic process. And an unstable one. Having you there as another pole created between us a field that felt charged and torqued.

JJ: Yes, the poems we read certainly had their charge, across so many areas of feeling and form! As for expectation, I think you have to accept that any editor will read poems through lenses such as reputation, or newness, and for sure they will 'hear' a poem through the voice of a poet they have heard read at this or that venue, or have read often on the page. And also welcome a 'voice' that's completely new or unexpected. Given that quite a number of these poems are from poets who've never yet been in this 'best of', and are by poets I've never personally met or heard read though I may have read on the page, and possibly you've not encountered 'live' either, shows that those accruals of reputation are complicated and can be inflected in various ways.

NL: I was really buoyed to learn that more than a third of the poets whose work we'd picked were first-timers in this series.

JJ: Yes, I was also happily surprised. Shows that it was ultimately about the poems, the words in front of us. Sure, poets want their work to be known, and reputation can derive from that. And many of these poems were already public and, clearly, even the unpublished poems we were sent are ones the poet wants published. This is public performance in one way or another. We see it, hear it, feel it. It may seem peripheral but being out in public accrues more than simply the lines, in this instance, on a page.

NL: It's really interesting, what you say about publicness, about the publicness of these poems, whether or not they've been published. They've been offered. And an offering, to my mind anyway, presumes a relinquishment of control over how the offering may be received. Perhaps it even expects, even accepts that whoever's receiving it can only do so while being blown about by all these contexts—some known to the offerer, some unknown.

In the guts of that—what stands out, and why? I don't know! I think ultimately I was persuaded by what I felt to be the attitude behind the poem, behind a line or turn or word cluster. An attitude of what? Maybe of a poem being simultaneously aware of itself as world-made and language-made? Of a poem understanding that nothing inside it escapes language—and revelling in that—while still trying to convey something—all the things!—outside of language?

I don't know! How about you?

JJ: Poems, or good ones, if I may use that term, are about change. I really reacted to this line, challenging or re-examining what we expect from subjectivity, from Dominique Hecq: 'This is how the I unwrites itself from the poem' ('Otopos'). Or the fantastic bluntness of 'I do not accept your politeness' from Amanda Anastasi's 'Monostich X: Glimpses'. So many of these poems created a sense of change, surprise, the struggle with language as it turns, or a curiosity about something, like an object, event, place, state of mind, and how that is never stable or one thing. They may be cheeky or serious, revelatory or satirical, formed obliquely, said plainly, just plain happy or sad, but there was something unexpected in the turn, something that made me stop.

NL: Beautifully said, and let's take that as a perfect place for us to stop.

✻

We thank all the poets who published or wrote poetry during the timeframe, whether their work appears here or not. We could have made this a longer volume as many surprising, beautiful, provocative, clever, energetic and/or eccentric poems could not, finally, be included due to space requirements. There were also poets whose work we may have expected to see but didn't, as it wasn't, so far as we know, published or written during the allotted timeframe.

We would like to thank Australian Poetry, in particular Jacinta Le Plastrier and Jennifer Nguyen, for all their work in supporting our reading and deliberations. They have been unfailingly patient and generous in their care for this volume. Thanks too to cover designer Sophie Gaur and designer and typesetter Chris Edwards for making the final volume look so wonderful in print, in the hand, for reading pleasure.

During the last year some poets have sadly passed away. We would like to honour the lives and careers of Charmaine Papertalk Green, Miriel Lenore, Jan Dean, Jennifer Chrystie, Moya Costello, and Jess Knight, and encourage readers to continue to seek their work. Our apologies if we have missed other passings.

Now it is up to you, dear readers, to 'feel for the shape of a poem' as Luke Patterson writes in 'Two Poems Shot on iPhone'. To discover new work that will provoke, pleasure, possibly perplex or unsettle in the many ways poetry does and has done always.

—*Jill Jones and Nam Le*

Contents

POEMS

2 stanzas from (outer spacings) | *PAM BROWN*

everybody loves
    the g chord
lifting up from c
to melaleuca
flower megrim
like a useless balm
that drapes the air
on roadworks corner

\- - -

clean the dust
from a little chunk
of crystal quartz
&
pocket it
to restore
an easy exit
from a valley
of ancient shrubs
when tipping point
drops low pressure
planetary waves
that turn anger
into sorrow
in a second

18 (*from* We Speak of Flowers) | EILEEN CHONG

the paintings we bought   of the interior
of someone else's   home now come across

as somewhat ironic   such black and white
it seems   do we know when to unmask

ourselves   how far should we stand
from those we love   gloves make

for poor intimacy   I caught sight
of a man at his desk   by a window previously

always shuttered   he saw me sweating
on my exercise machine   dressed in only a chemise

I was ashamed

I heard the music next door   and thought
of our ex-neighbour who loved   spanking

we would listen through the walls   and wonder
who was hurting the most   there are people

sitting on park benches   their eyes follow me
I worry   they can tell I am Asian underneath

ticker tongues send out   numbers in the thousands
sites crash and burn   your colleague

has curious taste in art   she gets up
sits inside the closet   I feel lucky

I am childless   dream about jars and wake to
measure   rise not descend write it down

the sun is watery   we have missed the summer
do leaves even fall   if you are no longer a witness

& whatever the man called each living creature, that was its name
| XIAOLE ZHAN

When Cangjie invented writing,
the sky rained with millet

& the ghosts wailed in the night,
fearing their actions may now be condemned

by the written word. I understood, too,
as a child who was beaten

out of love, what it means
to become a consequence. How

I came to recognise love
as revenge. How I hurt my mother

by hurting myself. Do you know
in Chinese the word for meat is

the animal? Say *beef*, you call *cow* 牛, followed
by the word *meat* 肉. If your daughter were

butchered, would you call her flesh
by her name? When I was a child

in Aotearoa, my mother read with me
every night *The Very Hungry Caterpillar*. When

we got to the very long list at Saturday, I wasn't
so much reading as memorising shapes

& sounds. When does remembering
become reading? Or is reading a kind of re-

membering over & over? It wailed for forty
days, forty nights & the broken ark was gap-

toothed with light. My childhood piano grazed
in my Pākehā grandmother's garden among the

ruminants, dromedaries, somnambulists. Foxs-
kin grinned & glistened, drawling the horizon. I

rose 塊 like a ghost 鬼 between two trees 林,
魔 summoned by karakia. I dreamt as a king 王

bitten hollow by moths, four mouths 口
in an endless scream 嚚. See, before things had

names you would just draw. Clot, jewel,
pomegranate seed all the same. Swallow

chocolate cake, pickle, lollipop, ice-
cream & call it *Saturday*. The oldest

words were beaten into oracle
bones. Remember & dis-

member. The word

for name 名 comes

from dusk 夕 &

mouth 口. O how

we call for each other

in the dark. O be-

fore name was

named I o-

pen-

ed my

dusk

mouth

& called —

for

-est; for

-get; for

you

After Heimat, *a Film Series by Edgar Reitz, 1984*
| *JENNIFER HARRISON*

Heimat is about leaving and returning
—EDGAR RITZ

          About bric-a-brac schools
       and milk curdling in thick glass bottles—
about dating apps and augmented reality
      about sisters and sons and the future—

         about Fontaine and fables
       illustrated by Gustave Doré
about the sick lion and the fox
      tracks going into a cave but none coming out—

         about ceasefires and the return of hostages
       drone bombs   thumb-struck—
about empty dresses
      celebrity and civilised fountains—

         about violence and families
       the construction of new train stations
of unerasable horror—
      about ducks flying in triplicate

         on a grandmother's loungeroom wall—
       about the many leather suitcases of the dead
car keys   garages   and accidental alarms—
      about leaving and returning   everywhere

Altered | ELFIE SHIOSAKI

come with me!
on a tin can rocket ship
jet propelled with escape velocity into an altered universe
 ESCAPE!

daydream with me!
at the edge of our universe
90 billion light years away

 there is a time and place called What Could Have Been

where the sovereignty of the Noongar Nation is unvanquished
the fresh water of the beeliar is unpolluted
and our children sleep
 with deep breaths of uninterrupted peace
 PEACE!

and there are rainbows, kittens and lollipops floating without gravity in space
 KITTENS!

it is nice here!

it did not have to be this way

Captain James Stirling, you did not have to reach for your pistol or sword
you could have reached for the compassion in your heart
                    the desire to tread lightly on Noongar boodja, without
                    trampling the spider orchid flat

our children need to know

            that it never had to be this way

An inventory of longing | KEVIN BROPHY

'The soul is looking for us, talking about us, where are we?'

In the after-vapours of a thousand wars
comes memory's need to be sure

what this passing quarky peace is for,
what longing it is now that fits its days –

memories return stunned from cities of ash
holding up a household spoon, swift smooth spoon

that longs for a world of lips,
and its shining cousin of forkish dreams

that swoop, pierce, fly into split-open mouths;

count within this peace among all there is
common carpet too, always made of stuff that's smoky,

thin, trampled-in, dull, and nervy
as a child laid out in a school infirmary;

and doors, whose faces long for locks,
whose pleasure's a tangle of bells in your head,

doors in thrall to the clawed-in fingers of hinges,
blind doors become yearning slaves to magic handles;

memories still know the silent knife, medieval tongue,
laid in the jaw of a kitchen drawer, eager

for its brighter, sleeker, keener Samurai
self, a mastery its stillness longs for,

steel-lit scabbards and unreeling emperors
whose sunlit eyes are cases of knives

whose tongues are dark thrills in their throats,
whose bodies made from old trampled carpets

consume breakfasts of blood through golden straws
as they squat each morning at tables too baroque

to straighten their painted legs –

the dictators condemned each day to ignore
the after-vapours of forgotten nightmares,

standing lost in palaces beneath towers of doors
(kindergarten cyclones in their furious fists),

no creamy spoon to take a lake's meniscus
at trembling lip,

no poddy-cheeked spoon, carrying spoon,
spilling spoon, spoony cornucopia, no such kitchen thing

that knows with all its longing the meeting of lips
in loveful concurring that the world is for sure

worth rolling whole in the mouth.

Apocalypse wears the ocean as if a dress
| SCOTT-PATRICK MITCHELL

after Saeed Jones

Apocalypse wears the ocean as if a dress.
Uriel sighs, dusts of his galoshes. Mount

Ararat prepares for landing. Somewhere, Noah
calculates how many more cubits of gopher wood

will be needed to accommodate the thousands
of new species discovered while Naamah, his wife,

shivers. She still has not rid the smell of manure
from linen. After her first miscarriage, Moonchild

tried on different religions as if they were skin.
None of them fit. From church to cathedral

to temple to synagogue to Tower of Silence,
she searched vaulted ceilings for an answer

to the ache, the clot, a future that refused
to stick. No angels or deities replied to her

cries. Desperate, she read The Bible, back
to front, fell in love, first with The Flood,

then with The Book of Revelations. One
phrase in particular stuck: *world without*

end. This, hope amid the grief. When Moonchild
tells you these stories, she reminds you that memory

is the shortest route to love. How she chose names,
but you never speak them, lest you are haunted: in her

world, superstition is a form of faith. The empty space
where a tree should be. In all the movies, *unto the ages*

of ages, cataclysm speaks. You check the sea levels,
elevation, calculate the time it would take for a wave

to break. To drown you all. In death, she says, you can
hold your breath. Forever. And then some. Moonchild

dreams, she tells you how Saint Catherine of Alexandria
leans in as Archangel Gabriel rocks his arms, shushes.

When you ask her how she thinks the world will end,
she points seaward, toward the horizon, and Apocalypse

picks up the ocean, wears it as if it were a dress
and, as she spins, seawater gushes down her legs.

when you and I were born couldn't the stratosphere have been a drug
we took to circle each other, orbiting in the way of seasons so that we
landed in the same hemisphere? wasn't earth shaped so there were no
years between us and the distance meant we could cross stars and skies
to reach each other? wasn't infinity a track we could cross to merge
in space? couldn't we find a way to travel without knowing a place of
nation or state? weren't telescopes that peer built to bring us closer?
couldn't universes collide so that we met before you fell to someone
else? didn't satellites navigate paths to bring us to unison? couldn't we
contract time so that when we missed we were led back towards each
other and the moon switched places with the sun so that what was
eclipsed didn't matter? weren't comets aligned with your name and
mine etched on them in the tiniest of atoms? didn't the earth's surface
endow us with language so that words could sing and the curve of our
letters embrace? weren't the coordinates our metaphor?

we were stretched across land and sea, our homes a journey meeting
in currents, swimming you to me and me to you. we were tracts of
land separated by history and bodies melded to one another before I
knew you. I heard your name the day I wrote this.

Autofiction | ŠIME KNEŽEVIĆ

The author composes an homage
to a self who sings and sails
on the great game of once upon a time.

I am a sailor. I sing to excess.
I am as perverse as degenerate art.
I typecast myself across digital space.

I am ageing with the superrich.
We go way back to the Ancients.
We even go to the same gym.

I sketch a shoreline, slowly
lifting the world, so it has days and
very soon the smell of lavender.

I 'feel' no separation between
aspects of my contents, a century
of classes, visits and titles. I feel intact.

My wounds reoccur in name only
where an encyclopaedia expands my body
until it touches the whole world.

I am also linked without proof
to my disappearance at lunchtime.
I summon a .wav file, and I sink.

A jaw-dropping way
to hide in continuous desire.
I am thrown into a fate where

I become an anonymous user with
a span of life as long as noon.
I am as calm and confused as the sea.

I signal with my hand.
I think it's a natural gesture.
A voice mirrors, so I speak

English. I feel any other school of
thought will try to silence me.
The feel of a daydream is like

the feel of a ripple in the ocean.
I am a ship in distress at sea.
I cry for mankind.wmv

A visitor | *BONNY CASSIDY*

<pre>
                    I have a
habitat that possesses me
that I overlook.   *Do you look after*
it?   Born so late in natural
history I look after everything. Take care,
caretaker, I said to myself
</pre>

— ROBYN SCHIFF, 'A Hearing', *A Woman of Property*

You had stopped telling stories about the present and future.
And because of this, you forgot them.

I spent my years narrating the past, burbling a mouth full of time.

Could I go into the forgotten days and recall them, set them in a line,
I wouldn't choose to. I say now, let it recede into a rare fold. I have
gone back and left it there and you will never find it.

I am not kin of this country. This is not a crisis.

It provides to me as it does to you. It has needs, too, it asks of me.

Here now, at dusk, it is asking me to turn down the lights; accept that
a shade becomes a silhouette then a surface for sound to bounce off or
ingest. Now is the time for the leaping and jerking creatures and you
must let them cross the night. Hush little storyhead it says, and I fall
into a dreamless sleep.

This is not a myth.

In this night something hunts and works that has been spoken of for ages, gone at daybreak somewhere higher. I find what it leaves in the hills, the gullies.

I strip my fear to bones, it seems real enough and fair. The feet are attached, untouched. The rest I pile up on a tome of slate well away from my dwelling.

This is not a dream.

In this country I began to get littler and bigger, sometimes on the same day. Patterns – dense, frayed – began to loom. Not metaphors.

I could be doing a lot of things with words. I could be making desperate whitefella magic, dancing with my haunted self, etc.

I ask more than this country can give, it asks only what I can. Sometimes I feel that I can't and then I hear it laughing at me. Laughter is breath.

On the hilltop something bright as a cockatoo appeared right at the edge of the forest, against the place where the pasture ceases to exist. It's still there. If a white bird is dead it will shrink and fall in a couple of weeks. If a plastic bag catches today's wind I'll no longer see it fixed there. If a warning sign remains upright, announcing the limits of enclosure, I am grateful. If a still orb holds my gaze for a night I will ride out to meet it.

You don't really want to destroy this country, but you are terribly afraid of failure. Terribly afraid. It is not nostalgia.

Look at all your lives; stepping around you, letting themselves

Axe Marks in Tree Trunks | NATALIE DAMJANOVICH-NAPOLEON

After the stories of Ljube Pavlinovich and Remy Beus[1]

To find my way home dad marked trees with an axe.
In the cut, tree trunks bleed amber lollies of sap,
pliant and malleable as 'girl,' a figure in wax.

At nine I dance five miles through bush, trunk to phalanx,
leaf to fingertip. School the crack of one handclap.
To find my way home dad marked trees with an axe.

Won a scholarship – my view through the lens, error parallax –
only boys were allowed an education. Caught in a mantrap,
became pliant and malleable as 'woman,' a figure in wax.

Re-shaped with knives, pliant hands, peculiar English syntax.
Girls only left home when they married – a ring entrapped;
to find my way home dad marked trees with an axe.

Fired in the kiln of tradition and culture, no longer clay or wax,
Hardened and breakable, I long for the days I was that
pliant and malleable 'girl,' a figure in wax.

"We need you at home," so I stayed, lived a life of anti-climax.
Who knew my life was a gift for me to unwrap?
To find my way home dad marked trees with an axe.
Who was that pliant and malleable 'girl,' a figure in wax?

1. These women's oral histories were recorded and collated by May Butko and posted
   on the Croatians in WA website at https://croatiansinwa.com.au/arts/women-in-
   wa/ Permission has been given by Butko & the Villa Dalmacia Assoc. to use the
   interviews.

Because a wind blazes
through the soft hands of autumn
I let the hurricane burn
against my heart.
What else are we to do
with all this anger?
The world will end &
we will let it.

•

Every day a kiss is stolen
by one stranger
from another.
Every day a building
comes down
on a child.

They call this being
unalived.

•

This is the world that we are making:
Not everyone gets
to smell thyme on their fingers
or to cook a simple dish
for the one who holds
their heart.

Not everyone gets
a life in roses,
nor even in crumbs.

•

Yesterday I saw wild horses
graze a hillside, in the fog.
They could not look at me
nor me at them
for shame.

•

Men tell me that some of us
are worth avenging;
some of us are human
animals.

This is a logic
I've heard before,
having once stood
in a zoo & been fed
to lions.

•

The world grows small in rain
but does not stay that way.

•

Because after autumn there are
other autumns,
we learn to eat the wind.
This is what we shall do
with all our anger.

Eat the wind &
spit it out.

•

Sometimes the waves
will rise so high in our mouths
they'll flood out
and drown windfarms
off the coasts of rich
& modern countries.

Sometimes we'll open
our chests &,
teeth first,
throw ourselves
from great heights.

Do not mistake us.

This is the world &
we will take it.

•

This is the longest moment ever.
And this one.

And this

Note: This poem references Israeli Defence Minister Yoav Gallant's words, 'human animals' in reference to Palestinians. The stanza following refers to Serbian propaganda spread in the lead up to the Bosnian war. Bosnian Muslims were accused of feeding Serb babies to lions in the Sarajevo zoo. As with the false claims that Hamas beheaded forty babies, this disinformation was used as a justification for the genocide that followed. The poem also adapts a few lines from Philip Schaefer's poem 'Suture'.

Birthplace | DAVID ISHAYA OSU

home:

      both sides of the avocado are on your mind / yearning for jamboree
      we will pass through the colon and return / with four fawns
      eating a cake sideways slows my life / heading to a riverbed
      is responsible for our voices / telling a phoenix
      all your names mean nothing / to the clay pot carrying your water

zero:

      the ribbons were there. he was taken out of redbuds. flesh of her flesh
      candlewicks think of you before they burn before you think of yellow
      slightly longer than a stream is listening to you & me fuck at all times

      taking tablecloths as family you look into the camera & climb lindens
      before losing your oldest coat you had had tea with purple potatoes &
      banged a door to the face of a trying day & went into a red floral wrap

eros:

      the blue light   in a lobby.
        asking   for a wet napkin.
          the moon   is not oversized.
                enough is not enough.
                in a bottle   of still water.
                  take your dream home.
                window   to window.
            a tight song is on   you, my friend.
                      for the sake of closets.
                 i have   just a day to tell.

Bogong song | MIRIEL LENORE

Mount Nelse North
    is higher
than Mount Nelse

Little Arthur
  overtops
Mount Arthur

Tawonga South's
   a town
of streets and lights

Tawonga just a
   thickening
of the road

the afterthought
   is not
the lesser thought

which

could be some
comfort to
the daughters of Eve

Brink | KATE LILLEY

I am a woman of the last century
a connoisseur of cupboards and compartments
answers reversed, a tangle for trembling ears
secrets of imitation exposed

a connoisseur of cupboards and compartments
letters of courtship and expired unguents
secrets of imitation exposed
glottal chink, botched frontispiece

letters of courtship and expired unguents
rima vestibuli, unversed speech
glottal chink, botched frontispiece
grosgrain ribbon stretched taut

rima vestibuli, unversed speech
a dewy bower open and shut
grosgrain ribbon stretched taut
the part when writing intercedes

a dewy bower open and shut
consent as extralegal
the part when writing intercedes
confessio amantis unto Venus and Cupid

consent as extralegal
answers reversed, a tangle for trembling ears
confessio amantis unto Venus and Cupid
I am a woman of the last century

Che Guevara Plants A Tree In Ceylon

| S. NIROSHINI

Transactions take place in each lover's consciousness

Like when he says *I love you*, he means *I love those parts of you that cut my dark*

The empire used indentured labourers from South India
on its coffee, tea and rubber plantations in the 19th century

[To search for another word for *empire*]

In Kalaripayattu when the leg makes a circular kicking action outwards
it is described as *puram*. When the motion is inwards: *agam*

Agam: the interior landscape, or love poetry, in Tamil from the second century BC

What he said: I want to make love to you again
and again in a thunderstorm

It was a mahogany tree that Guevara planted, once upon a time in Ceylon

Once upon a time is a lazy translation of the Tamil *ore oru oorile...in that one
and only town*

What he said: I want to know language
that bites with its specificity

'*His favourite garden in the world had been the grass garden at Kew, the colours
so delicate and various*'

Guevara had been part of a trade delegation from Cuba.
His glamorous interpreter stood next to him in a black and white photograph

To search for the interpreter's name without success

Puram: the public domain, the praise of kings, poets and war

'And there is yet another Cuzco, a vibrant city whose monuments bear witness to the formidable courage of the warriors who conquered the region in the name of Spain....'

Before love, before war, there was—

Screaming is an effective way to reduce the experience of pain

And pain, like all cycles in nature, longs for its completion

Notes:
'His favourite garden in the world...' is from *The English Patient* by Michael Ondaatje (1992).
'And there is yet another Cuzco...' is from *The Motorcycle Diaries* by Ernesto Che Guevara (1992).

Chinese Funerals as Theatre | XIN LEE

Five days have felt like forever,
which is how long a widow could spend
folding a kingdom of joss papers.
Yesterday we burned my father a mansion,
a Mercedes, an iPhone, and charger.
Today, three monks in a funeral parlour,
three prayers for a non-believer,
and a mockery of the Chinese vernacular.
Tomorrow, there will remain only a son,
his mother, and one half of her daughter.

Cordon Sanitaire | ADAM AITKEN

Where the plantations begin.

The scent of the earth, the true-born.
A foot on the earth, your earth.
An electrified fence to keep the cows from straying.

A line of sanity
or sanitation, the city limits once defined,
the streets washed in lime & lavender.
The balconies overflowing with roses.

The end of reason or the beginning
of purer emotions, the line
between fear & mobilised ambition.
But will an ocean protect us?

At the local fête I asked Sandi from Atlanta
why she came here. More relaxed she said,
good ideas appear more often.
No Trumpist here. Just us Democrats
making France great again (joke).
She and Honey had the paperwork in control.

She convinced me as we queued
at a burger van, for the European kind
which *were* better,
with their black buns real tomato sauce
& purple bull flesh.
They had a regional status, she said, so
French, everything
a bit raw, fragrant, & safe to eat.

Corpus mundi | HELEN SWAIN

Once, kneeling on lino
in the passage by the kitchen
she was mouth-wide ready

to receive God concealed
in plastic discs
of tiddlywinks chosen

as Christ-like
for practising goodness.

Afterwards the real host
pulled moisture from a patch of tongue.
her inside cheeks leaked.

Teeth parted to prevent biting
baby Jesus before
he was made into part of her make believe,

swallowed,
body and soul incorporated,
girl child with God power.

Him and her close like held up fingers
crossed, steepled.

Craig fugue | ALICE ALLAN

Canberra, 2002

I was 20, rich, & lying
on my Newstart
so I could buy us petrol,
maybe drinks
at Das Kapital,
where we once saw Kim Beazley,
who'd just lost the election
post-Tampa, post-9/11.
I had this sweet office gig
making photocopies,
answering phones.
Mum's neighbour Craig
ran the café across the road.
He gave us freebies.
My boss loved Craig
& his coffees.
Her daughter rang the office
at least twice a day.
Hanging up,
my boss would say:
"Don't get married.
Don't have kids."
My Newstart got us
a converted garage
with a sloping bathroom
& under-floor millipedes.
We snuck in a kitten.
Craig had two kids
plus a wife on mat leave.
He checked on Mum.

Mum loved Craig
& his two kids.
Kim Beazley promised
he'd make Les Murray
poet laureate
as soon as he was PM,
but Labor dumped Kim
the same week his brother died.
Les died later.
Craig moved out.
Das Kapital
is an açai place.

'…the two-headed man has half as much of twice of everything'
—BRUCE BEAVER, 'Letters to Live Poets (XII)'

    i.

after // hearing a weird biracial
insult directed at your back //
you search memories using facial

recognition // gawking at diss track
escalations in the soundclouds
(cirrus & serious) // these slack

conversations drop their shrouds
over us // always predictive always
productive // stock photos of crowds

inhabit the present // new days
establish themselves like an optionless
future // you're obvs-asian through the haze

   through the login details of the windless

,

ii.

afternoon // summer continues with
prayers encrypted into these leaves
& with parks that appear on the fifth

trip around the block // part of you believes
all terms & conditions are systematic
theologies in disguise // what else receives

such grateful assent? // the apophatic
profits pay out when any device
loses its attachments // the static

of sparrowsong is data's hidden price //
these seasons just autoplay don't
they? // you've got to click twice

   to prove you're no robot // won't

,

iii.

you include all ethnicities from the out-
set next time? // the city's passing faces
form an unsatisfactory playlist // doubt

is its own lock screen // uncertainty graces
each password attempt // the financial
year will end like a catechism with traces

of old arguments // & substantial
rmb gains (o those gains) // when did you
log in & tamper with the circumstantial

avarice? // yeah that's not a new
crime // that's not even hidden // the ad
follows your wandering eyes through

these circles: thumbprint, watchface // bad

,

iv.

advice now transposed into a singable
bak cham gai recipe // you accepted everything
when you signed up // e.g. winnable

arguments that must always cling
to doubly-inhabited premises //
when a roast duck quacks it's another ring-

tone non-echo myth // he menaces
you & it goes straight to voicemail //
he fashions a sixteenth-note nemesis

from a dummy account // fail-
proof plan // man // hi-hat
pattern you love but can't nail //

transcribing the new year// chopping white chickens // & all that.

Dementia | *ANNA KERDIJK NICHOLSON*

My friend again loses a word,
momentarily absents herself,
staring at her meaning as if struck
by holiness, by her gilded icons,
caught in a vision, pictorial and complete
into which her glottal stop sounds
and her eyes, flickering like altar candles,
reluctantly turn from clarity,
without liturgy,
unable to complete the response.

sometimes it's just a need/want to touch yr face
extend a leg on couch, plant foot arch to hip
watch a frangipani or a pickle or a gentle theory grow.
a car alarm wakes me from this place. this peak of day
starts a galah to remind me where I am
a hum from the kettle, from the Speak Easy Neighbour
the turny ungrounded, the platte spins, a Lazy Susannah
searches for her Purpose or a mushroom.
the pigeon in pumps beats it past this window
yr skin as you adjust to yr cold mourning shower

sometimes it's blackout blinds drawn at midday
just myself, sweet horizon, prone to making terrible decisions
I pool a wetness out of mind. we're both prone, somewhere,
u & I. a past summer still presses at my thighs
yr past winter recalls snow / falls like tinnitus,
pulsing a soft, grey reminder; dampness marks
the season change. an ibis expands wings, launches
in south-east winds & we keep this gesture,
as we flirt like friends & remain so—better whole
& alight than broke like a window,

                            venetians flappin in the wind

direct to ashfield | ALISON WHITTAKER

edging on eleven pm
a train pulls up, direct to ashfield

it's been raining
things not worth mentioning, but
lights replying to themselves
for however long the rain lifts

i want to understate it so bad.

an empty train, yellow inside
the opposite of an orgasm
ah, whatever,
bewildered in the dark, rooted in place

i want to understate it so bad.

redfern station, december in a hard year
terminal, never seen it before.

i've been in tears on and off
there's a split in the pressure of the air tonight
in platform puddles, they can do this
offers this, a small stillness to see.

slowing gradually, stopping quick
but kind of like one, in its pace?
i feel like i've cum
pulsing, agape.

every unwashed window has these
abandoned hairs from commuters
a day of human stink, visible like this
because on my sad and briefly still night
their stained glass window, kind of
prints of grease
resting their heads
only because the source left and
its cavern illuminated me and to me
their chorus their chorus, kind of.

i step on the train
it carries me, not quite to home
for strangers' pain
i think i'm the only one
overwhelmed with a terrible love
for ghosts.

i tell the friends who will listen
and if they listen as i tell them
this sweaty train, how it hit me.
how it hit me, that they love me.

i want to understate it so bad.

Distance | FELICITY PLUNKETT

I am anyone
who set the table for two
and ate alone.

Who watched lamplight
soften a winter
window from the lone dark.

Wore a face
down with low
things she had known.

Anyone who paced
at night to hold
the world in place.

Stood her ground, far
from a hand, laughter
close in a room's glow.

Outside, followed
clouds' roll
towards pink, fold

into mauve. Saw night's
roses open to a close
moon's glister. This

is where she was inside – this
vast archive, its ceilingless
marvel, its stars.

My Day According to Me: Moods—everywhere! I am asking my desolation for analysis; it happens in every poem. Better get drinking! My fridge is full of bad energy. Outside, I'm struck by a demented egg yolk of sun. No one plans for these to become their days. I peruse my library of habits. Every day I am getting better (at drinking). According to my mood analysis, mood is everywhere. But ask *me* or *my poems* and I go, with splendour, into the wrong document. Slabs of feeling erupt from spreadsheets, bills, emails—I'm budgeting for an adult that doesn't exist. The world has shrunk to the size of my body and increasingly I don't like what goes on in there. Last time an emotion happened I needed a doctor and he told me to write 'analysis day'; it's getting better every mood. But me? Ask my drinking poems. I am everywhere according to my desolation.[i] Long and sluggish lines flop into the kitchen and I get busy installing air quotes around helpful advice. At this stage all books are burn books. I've been going to mass all year: I genuflected at the tabernacle (box), figured out what the foot cushions are for (knees), didn't mean to take the Jesus snack (communion). God, do you stick a finger in every now and then? Prayer: What does it mean to let go? God, please, take my collection of objects, my empties, and transform them into the communion of subjects. Don't let me be alone.

[i] Simone Weil, a connoisseur of affliction, names four evidences of mercy down below: 1. the experience of god; 2. the radiance and compassion of some who know god; 3. the beauty of the world; 4. the complete absence of mercy here. Is this what rock bottom looks like?

Eleven Portraits of Drowning | MADELEINE DALE

A hundred and ten millimetres in a single day.

Local bridges were cut quickly –
a decade ago, they still followed fording paths,
low-slung concrete kissed by shallow creeks.

It used to seem good luck to be shut in by water,
to seek alternate routes   miss appointments.

~

A list of drowning victims:

Natalie   found spine-up in the Pacific,
              the downed bird of her jacket snatched
              from its element.

Two men argued politics over her absence;
the coroner wrung water from her clothes
– and no-one could clear it from her lungs.

~

A river in flood is spoken like a pregnancy:
swollen swelling hungry banks broken broken waters.

Our words for birth are our words for fear.

~

                    Two men found upright in
Ophelia's   grave –
                    she swallowed her death in the dry impasse
                    between scenes five and six. Men argued

over her mind as she stepped out of the text
and into the water.

                              ~

A search for drowned women:

drowning porn videos drowning underwater videos
drowning watch women drowning porn videos for free.

                              ~

It's not the water.

                              ~

The Australian Border Deaths Database:

Interdiction at sea   *2 women*   *4 adult women*
1 female (pregnant)   *three female children*
Unknown woman   *small number of women*

142 women.

                              ~

An immigration minister is sixty per cent water.

~

Christina   in nine inches of fire-stung stream,
                     wet eyelids, soot skin.
                     Two men argued over the story –

and no-one remembers who lifted her out of the water
or swept a billow of soaked hair from her temple.

~

Ruin takes record for challenge; the interior
of any lung is a ready site of inundation.

What to carry? When to tie back our hair
and place our names in a water-tight tub?

A coal baron is sixty per cent water.

~

Three point two millimetres in a single year. Two men
argue over how high the Pacific will take a tidemark

on a sitting-room wall   on a high-rise   a feed-shed
over a field   a river system   a freeway   a damp shirt.

A woman sits down in a flood of salt.

Entry Wound | BRONWYN LEA

It came through the back fence –
a wound shaped like air learning its name,
a fold in the paddock where the grass leaned inward,
and the dog stepped back, jaw closed, eyes fixed,
and the shed light held at the hinge,
and I stood at the sink, one hand inside a wet sleeve,
as the wound arrived – a cry with aim,
sharp as a key dropped edge-first through the body,
and it struck once, behind the ribs,
then settled clean beneath the breastbone,
and the house continued –
cup on the bench, shirts dripping –
but the grammar had changed,
and the world began to tilt around that wound,
and the cry – if cry is the word – held open the spine
until the bones began to listen.
From that moment the sentences followed,
each one reaching toward what had already spoken.

Epistolary | JO LANGDON

'Sometimes this life here seems unreal … precisely because it's purely corporeal'
—ALINA SZAPOCZNIKOW TO RYSZARD STANISŁAWSKI

This pen writes beautifully, it's just that I lie
wrong, and from this position the letters come

out crooked. Hospital life, the smell of ether,
of disinfected filth. Everything is white &
aquamarine, even I am

light blue (insipid). But just beside me there,
life: lovely, desired, anticipated. And nearby

very red, almost glowing
little roses, and you
are there again.

Coffee with milk, very good
bread with jam, peaches. The room is lovely,
clean, a radio, around

20 young women: 3 maids, a nurse etcetera.
Meanwhile you

no doubt are already sprouting
angel's wings (check
above your shoulder blade).

[soft pencil girl with braids]

Note: this poem is comprised of textual fragments from the artist Alina Szapocznikow's letters
to Ryszard Stanisławski, first compiled in the edited collection *Lovely, Human, True, Heartfelt:
The Letters of Alina Szapocznikow and Ryszard Stanislawski, 1948–1971* (2012), edited by Agata
Jakubowska and translated by Jennifer Croft, published by the University of Chicago Press.

Extinction song | ANDY JACKSON

I'm facing the horizon. Any edge of this headland, at a
　　　　　moment's notice (or less) can shear off. Disintegration
　　　is like this, gradual and sudden. Surge of cortisol, aria
　　　　　　　of a body shaken by its future. A more severe seizure

of reason is to imagine the death of another, a loved fellow walker
　　　　　through stressed, remnant country. These days, when solitary,
　　　I'm restless in remembrance and foreboding. An overdub I
　　　　　　　(and you) can discern in the human chorus. The full moon

can make light of darkness. How can we, when we're asynchronous
　　　　　　with our own heartbeat, with the earth? Each death strips
　　　a layer of skin off. (Wave follows wave, to break upon the shore.) Every life,

　　　　　every animal, a library, with the fires closing in. Our perch on jagged
circumstance, like staggering along a windswept cliff –
　　　　　　and smoke obscures the way to a vast, older garden.

Note: After Ryuichi Sakamoto (1952–2023).
The last words of each line are taken from the track titles of his album *async* (2017).

Fifteen ways to be erased
| *DAVID STAVANGER AND SAUL STAVANGER*

Note: In this co-written piece, the sections in [square brackets] are by Saul Stavanger; the non-bracketed sections are by David Stavanger.

'Our school rejects that all forms of bullying behaviours exist'

1.

We spend up to three years of our lives in the toilet. I was thirteen when I first started regularly hiding in them. I would make sure no one saw me enter and then pick the stall furthest from the door as long as it was clean (or clean enough), drawing my feet up on the closed seat, tucked tight so no teachers could sight legs during a sweeping check.

Toilets offer solace in ways some people find in an emptied church – a chorused silence, the metaphysical self disrobed, prayers formed from necessity and pursuit. By this stage the bullying had reached a level that led me to disappear regularly, in flux between domestic tensions and the hypervigilance of school, unsure as to what lay halfway but also knowing it was safer to be nowhere than either.

Bully*: third-person present.
Bully*: noun; corned beef.
Bully*: harasser of the weak; harasser of the week.
*If you write the word bully three times during this recollection, they will reappear in your bathroom mirror.

2.

[Physically hiding is my first form of hiding: things like bathrooms, cubicles, and outside of PE block are the kinds of places I can sit away from everyone else. Talking to teachers to avoid going out to lunch, taking different routes getting home to avoid certain people and situations. I first started hiding in Year 3, when I was eight. I used to hide up in the library. It was the only place in the school that had air-con.]

[My first mental hiding was books – fantasy books. I read a lot of books. That worked for a while until kids saw I had books on me, which worsened the bullying. Books in breaks solidified that I was a weirdo, an outsider.]

[I began world-building little towns, then cities, then made a country – the map was pretty terrible. Any free time I would dedicate to daydreaming or writing down any little or important events and timelines from this fictional universe when I couldn't talk to many people in my class. Created my first world – it had the illusion of a real world where I could hide. I didn't exist in these worlds; I just watched over them and decided what happened. School was a place where I couldn't be me.]

3.

Hi ██████

We are still not sure if we will take things further with the police. Unfortunately, outside of CCTV footage, there are no witnesses to the events.

I want to say how terribly sorry I am that this has happened to Saul.

I have every confidence that the school will deal with these boys seriously once they have been identified. However, I do think you should consider ██████'s suggestion that this be taken further with the police.

Which books did he lose?

Does he have any friends?

I hope this does not cause his social development to regress and his anxiety to increase.

Kind regards,

███ ███████

Learning Support

4.

I – and now my son Saul – have attended multiple schools due to bullying. Perhaps the education system hasn't really changed that much in thirty years. We are both experts at hiding, though theirs is more refined than mine. I read in the local paper that their previous high school has recently been part of a trial of school 'wellness' workshops where boys paint each other's fingernails while being taught about toxic masculinity, discussing self-harm and what it means to be a man. I think of the way my son bit their nails down to the skin while they were at that school, eating themself in front of me. The aim is for young blokes to see it's just paint. The same way we tell young kids it's just blood. Some parents have apparently slammed it as nutty and weird. I see them painting their children into a corner, and once cornered, those kids see red instead of stop.

5.

[Sometimes I would go and watch a bird's nest in the grounds. I would go there to both hide and read – and I liked the birds. One day some kids tried to smash the bird's eggs and I tried to stop them, but my opinion didn't really matter to them at all. My opinion never mattered.]

6.

I looked up reviews of Saul's last school on Google. Someone with the handle 'Jesus Sparklez' has written, 'If you wish the unhappiest education for your child. This is the place to go.' A better motto than the trinity of text nailed to the school's front gate: RESPECT × RESPONSIBILITY × INTEGRITY. It's a conceptual commitment at best. When my son was surrounded by dozens of students, being called a *faggot* after their 'friend' announced to the whole cohort that Saul identified as pansexual, the new guidance counsellor spoke at length about the school's supportive culture for queer kids and avoided the F-word in case saying it would manifest a faggot before him. Like to see that guidance counsellor de-escalate a fist at the point it regrades a face. Like to know the last time someone reduced him to a noun.

7.

[First time I was physically in danger,
I was walking home and one of my main bullies
started tailing me on his bike.]

[When we got back my bag it was turned
inside out ·
and my stuff was all over a field.]

8.

When Saul was assaulted walking to the station and on the train getting home from one school, the learning support team suggested that they arrive and leave before the bells, as they couldn't guarantee their safety. They don't even have bells anymore (whoever created the end-of-days mixtape, with its over-reliance on Alice Cooper, needs to know that school's never out for many kids.) We were told to go to the police; we were told Saul was sensitive and provocative. Adjectives are positioned to undermine victims (even the term 'victim' has an unspoken narrative of responsibility in schools, as if children assign themselves that role).

Saul started arriving at different times and entering the grounds covertly from a back path, their actions the result of education as a public institution, minimising harm to itself. One morning, they turned up to walk this path and smelt decay nearby, turned to see the carcass of a juvenile whale rotting on a reef off the beach at the end of their school's street. Onlookers gathered, keen to see the shark feeding frenzy. It's one of the first memories that springs to mind whenever we pass by their former school gate.

We withdrew Saul from that school the following month, towing them out into deeper water so they could float, leaving all the detritus of that year in the shallows.

9.

Saul and I watch *High Fidelity* and the next morning, knowing their love of lists and rating things, I ask for their Top Five* bullies:

[████o. Would attack me on the train. Spreading rumours. YR8]
[███n. What didn't she do. Told me to kill myself multiple times. YR8]
[█a█. Punched me in the face and started the homophobia stuff. YR7]
[██c██. Chased me home on a bike. YR5]
[███b. The taser person. YR3]

[*hard as there are quite a few, I can't remember all their names] I hear this as 'games'.

[The school counsellor advised me to ignore the name calling and it would go away—they were just nicknames. Sitting in a white room, low chromatic, at a wooden desk with a black chair. She didn't really listen—there is a certain way they speak that tells you they're not listening, offering the same advice as last time.]

10.

Hesitation marks appeared in the margins of my son's learning. They began to doubt words, even when they were written down or bolded in emails or on their own lips, shedding trust in language and that adults are licensed to name things as solid or known. Every adult, from year advisors to learning units to teachers to relatives to parents, became unreliable when they opened their mouths. Often, I felt I had nothing concrete to offer beyond our shared doubt.

11.

[I moved interstate. There was no bullying at my new school at first. I thought things were going to be great. Once my one friend left, it felt like no one wanted to be associated with me at all. Playing a game of tag, I was hiding behind a tree because I'm not a fast runner. These kids from the year above started making fun of me for being socially awkward (the teacher's phrase), and I cried. They grabbed my bag and took it into the toilets and threw it in the urinal. All my work was in it. Classwork, books, my world-building. Drenched. Ruined. Went and found a teacher, and I got detention.]

12.

I bump into a friend while taking my dog (and my doubts that I have anything meaningful to write about bullying) for a walk. She says 'Perfect – doubt is what bullying is all about.' All the ways it centres and amplifies doubt. Doubt of your child's take, their muscle memory and their written account. Doubt about encouraging your child to be empathetic towards the bully, doubt that the bully truly exists. Doubt that the school has it under control, doubt that they're taking it seriously, doubt that they have the mechanisms to manage what's happening out of their sight. Questioning where responsibility lies, who's telling the truth, the possibility that your child is somehow soft or you're not hard enough, or you're both too sensitive – the 's' word again, lodging itself in your subconscious as various non-parents recommend self-esteem tutorials or martial arts classes. For both of you.

One day, one of Saul's main antagonists said he had a taser in his bag and was going to use it on Saul. The school's response was to doubt that there was a taser or that the word 'taser' had been used. I wanted to obtain a stun gun after this. And use it on the other kid's parents. Who are probably full of another form of the same misplaced rage as I am. Not many parents talk about the violent fantasies that can play out after your own child is directly threatened or harmed. Stunning to look into the light of your child and see yourself burning.

13.

[Year 6 was really bad socially—isolating and kids making bad rumours about me, special rules for me to not be able to play handball, pushing me out the back. It was my only way to hang with other kids. I was very depressed. I felt suicidal, holding myself hostage under a desk with a knife to my wrist.]

[The most significant out of all the things people don't tell you about bullying is that being resilient doesn't solve the problem. When you're told that you're super resilient, it has the same effect as being told to ignore it and it'll go away. No matter how emotionally strong you are, having every aspect of your identity mauled by your peers will hurt.]

14.

You know there is no good–bad binary here: one of Saul's long-term bullies turned out to have a mother dying of cancer, another was experiencing regular beatings at home. In some ways, their victims were the most reliable intimacy they had in their lives, often one in which they had a sense of agency and control. The word 'bully' likely evolved in the mid-sixteenth century from the Middle Dutch word boele, which loosely translates as 'lover'. A term of endearment, a familiar form of address to an intimate friend. Often, a bully is the first person we are pursued by, the first person to make meaningful physical contact, the first to give us pet names, the first to fixate and to seek us out in times of shared confusion and doubt.

15.

[Bullying is a sea of faces, morphing and changing. Its only desire to consume lest it devour itself. Although it is always in a state of flux, it hates change, even more so difference, covering it with the oozing sludge of its toxicity. It is infectious and can transform even those who don't want to be consumed by it, while the fate of those who refuse to give in isn't much better—the sea of faces inspects every part of them and tears each one to pieces. The monster cannot be destroyed, as its faces are always changing.]

Coda

My son's advisor called me as I missed parent–teacher night. Fortunately, their latest school is a move away from 'appointment learning'. Their motto is *One student at a time, in a community of learners.* Teachers are advisors, parents are peripheral planets, students are agents of their own making. I still have a vigilance around school calls, built up through years of Saul being bullied or retaliating to bullying or being attacked and preparing myself to legally represent them. But this call was to tell me how Saul is thriving, how they lead the class discussions, how the world-building project they're working on is blowing minds, how Saul spends their time beta-testing friends' game designs and playing Catan in beanbags, that there is funding to support all the autism spectrum disorder kids in ways that can be defined by the kids themselves.

Saul hasn't been called a faggot or a retard this year. Hasn't been hit or kicked or spat on or told to kill themself. No bags emptied or books stolen. Catches public transport again. Wants to stay at their mum's on school nights so they can catch even more trains. New records. The faces don't appear so much in sleep now*, the night terrors have finally stopped, and there are soft reports that their dreams are slowly becoming their own.

*

[Among the sea of people, I spot the amorphous creature again. A colossal tide of echoing laughter washes over me, knowing it has already gotten the best of me.]

In the lead-up to Christmas, I take Saul to a foragers' market in the same suburb as their previous high school to find some final gifts. Saul's hesitant to go, given the geographic association and the potential hypervigilance they may need to negotiate. I reassure them that all that was twelve months ago, and they are safe with me. Saul isn't safe with me. While looking at handmade soap, I don't see Saul stiffen, face stripped of its natural colour. Saul comes up close, whispering in an agitated state that the bullies are over there but I'm not to look, *please don't look.* I look.

[I anticipate something happening and, in fact, hope for it so that this burning tension droning on in my brain will stop.]

Standing in a small, broken circle are Saul's past tormentors, openly mocking them across the stalls. Spoilt coal-coast kids, cruel mouths full of sweets. I hold the bath bomb in my hand tighter and stare back, as if a stare can dissolve their essential nature. Saul wants to leave, but I keep staring, fixed on a target that's not on my back. I buy a pomegranate bath bomb. Nothing explodes. We leave together and we walk away alone, unsure how to transcend this.

[I do not remember the time it took or how long he said it would take, I just remember it being an eternity to me.]

Flood Myth | GURMEET KAUR

What if tomorrow the great floods arrive
and seagulls migrate under dark skies
while the sun so much sun hurries out
of the way what if rivers shatter the banks
and swans disappear what if thick winds
descend and cranes stop washing in lakes
instead hover above glutted grounds, birds
unearthed, wait for storms to subside
while the gods are nowhere to be found
and when we think of the end what if we
imagine small bodies like millions of snails
crawl out of holes unfurl in mist by the
Maribyrnong, drink floodwater in drops,
work with the sun to lighten the living.

Note: After Gilbert White's *The Natural History of Selborne.*

'Living in the earth-deposits of our history'—ADRIENNE RICH

'No person shall do or omit to do anything that frustrates, hinders, interferes
with or derogates from the operation or implementation of the Indenture,
or any aspect of the Indenture, or the ability of the parties to the Indenture
or any other person to exercise rights or discharge duties or obligations under
the Indenture.'—*Roxby Downs (Indenture Ratification) Act* 1982

Extensions of Time

The morning coils into my body after I sit in the office chair
and I am again kneeling in the boot of a station wagon—floating
along the Olympic Dam Highway toward the Woomera Theatre.
Memories wail into fragments when acts and details are forced—
I cannot recall the movie, only the furious and howling gestures
of little bodies singing 'Achy Breaky Heart' by Billy Ray Cyrus.
From my conception—I pulse and merge into a binding energy
dispersing from this existence. Consider this account dependable
as if printed in books based on transcripts I extensively recorded
during my recently established career as a receptionist. I applied
for the advertised role, interviewed, and signed a contract for the
standard three-month probationary period after my references
were confirmed. The arrangement began to make sense, gradually,
but not gently, as I archived reports, took minutes, and fielded phone
queries to the relevant executives, et cetera. I envisioned a beautiful
future without the weight of a man expertly surveying me. It rains
every time he presses me against the ground and my body absorbs
into soil. This is why I ache and split every time you clear my touch
away from your arm—my fingers are too cold. I become raw material
preciously anticipating warm breath from an open mouth—no deeper
than a soul hopes to be, but as vast as the demountable accommodations
cemented for single men's quarters in this occupied zone. Sand dunes
were reported to be uninhabitable, ready to be fucked for what uranium
is to power. Copper to heat cities, fuelling generators, motors, lighting
fixtures, televisions, computers—almost anything electrical. Eureka—
I am a gold furnace and ready to smelt minerals in a state-of-the-art
facility as a bonanza of slurry swells for Australia's pipeline pioneers.

Liability of Joint Venturers

Billy is due to ride through town again, wearing his trademark denim jacket
and ready to clean the rooms of the Oasis Hotel. From his lips—to his fingertips,
Billy is more than just a brother to Kevin and Mick. He is my singing cowboy
personifying masculinity on stage. Billy knows how to strip and make a bed
deluxe with the measured rhythm of a line dance. Billy sways dignity beyond
the aloofness of mixing red dirt with booze. I want to tell Billy about this man.

Applicable Law

The Western Mining Corporation established a very special relationship with the South Australian government to arrange the Roxby Downs (Indenture Ratification) Act 1982. This legal framework permitted an exclusive licence for Western Mining to construct, maintain and operate a mine in the Olympic Dam Area—a compact but immensely rich ore body consisting of copper, gold, silver and the world's largest deposit of low-cost uranium. This joint venture in conjunction with the State—superseded the Aboriginal Heritage Act 1988, the Environmental Protection Act 1993, the Freedom of Information Act 1991, the Natural Resources Act 2004, the Development Act 1993, and the Mining Act 1971. Western Mining did not even register the presence of saltbush before extensive development occurred in 1986. More than a billion dollars has been spent advancing Olympic Dam's underground and surface operations to adhere to world-class standards. Teams of environmental scientists and health specialists regularly meet in a windowless room to audit and measure radiological impacts and prevent any calculable damage to the region's flora and fauna. This, along with stringent health and safety practices guarantees the well-being of workers driving home in their station wagons from the mine to drink and dwell in hundreds of air-conditioned houses. Growing families can only flourish in the purpose-built town of Roxby Downs—an oasis of modern civilisation. With an increasing global need for uranium, Olympic Dam's prospects as a supplier are as vast as the people working to extract it. Life is peaceful in this little township settled amongst the red sandhills. Given the facilities, services and opportunities available—Roxby Downs is Australia's most highly regarded mining town. As loudspeakers announce 'port' townspeople chant 'power'—melodic voices carry past the hour-and-a-half distance by plane to South Australia's capital city, Adelaide. Beyond the city's commercial business and retail facilities, it is famous for its European flavour and Mediterranean climate. Home to a booming wine industry and a thriving arts and cultural festival, held every two years, it is here that Olympic Dam's marketing headquarters is based—with expert salesmen busily exporting products to energy-hungry nations with the touch of a cold, damp hand. From mine to market, Olympic Dam's reputation as an economic and politically stable enterprise is refined from port to power and measured in centuries.

into a person.
Athena does this to Odysseus
in Phaeacia, in Ithaca
but we do not need a goddess
for this to take place.
She only helps us understand

what is already within us.
I can pour grace
into you: make you taller, younger, more formidable.
See your hair, it flows down in curls like hyacinth petals.
The years of trial and shipwreck
I have wiped them away.

you are bony as a flagpole.
when I wrap my arms around you
I can feel you flying half-mast.

your mother is black. your father is grey.
your siblings, all of them navy.

traffic horns play dirges here,
and women behind counters suck tongues
of stainless steel.

the borders are terrifying:
all those loaded bullets chafing
under the shade of bloated bread dough bellies.

once a man with a padlocked face barked:
go home. there's not enough water here.

after they let me in
they thrust a cicada between my legs.
it clicks and whirrs when I'm out on the street
and the men, whose myocardia possess a remarkable
refrigerating quality, circle.

Halfway Things | DAVID MUSGRAVE

i.m. Jordie Albiston (1961–2021)

On the outer reaches   drifting
where the summer sharpens
pacific glare on its own winnowing
currents   wavery graft of blades
strewn in prismatic deep   bladderwrack
on scripted foam deep in blue-green
homeward   resuming lime and lemon light
of tide

*

Had you never left
you'd be just here in the middle   yep
aslant and at a remove
but time has hoovered you up   yep
up and out into the cosmos.

*

This is the good place, of grass
plumping with rain, and liquidambar
seed pods like meteors burrowed by moonworms,
pebbly clay trickling with the slow runoff
of wind conducting the skitter-chorus of leaves,
suspiring pigface and gold-tipped orb-weavers
patiently cruciform   wasps embossing the leeward hollows
of dune-bedded rocks:
there is no other place, just places,
none better than this place, where you aren't.

Halfway things. Echo and abandon,
low stratus mizzling imperfection:

                                out of the horizon
of mortal thoughts, light disappears
into mottled yolk, livid-veined and bluish orisons
of refracted darkness. Slab-cold
wind picks off the defenceless spume.
Something older than fire
that inhabits all things at their core
leans into its work, a spoor
of damaged shapes, forgetful
that today is deeper than yesterday
but still as shallow as a shimmering puddle,
weird as a truckful of dewy-eyed camels
chewing sideways as they wobble over the bridge
at Waratah Station.

                        *

unspeakable joy   unspeakable
grief irrupts playfully   prolonging
itself   recalcitrant   rosaceous
clouds and the sun's disappearing self,
into nights that seem more permanent now,
more like a state of affairs arrived at
and agreed to   even announced as angles
of carpentry   mortice of coffin-boards,
dead flowers for the dead, flowering once more.

Hey Girl | THUY ON

Hey girl
Let's play MisAsianed!

Are you:
Filipino
Thai
Singaporean
Malaysian
Korean?

Did your mother mate with a GI Joe
cos you look like a halfie
eyes not quite power points
Kawaii round not shuttered slits
c'mon spark me in

Hey dumpling your lashes are garnish
eyes dark soy sauce
slip slip through my fingers like vermicelli
puckered mouth of chillies
oh you are blister-hot

Hey girl, your English is so good
no sing song ching chong lilt lisp
if only my ears saw you
nah yeah certifiably Aussie for sure
just hold the coriander ok?

Holocaust in the genocide | OMAR SAKR

The living and dead, my friends
And enemies, all are obscured
By millions of memories—
What some call human
Shields. Nobody has devised
A more complete weapon.

Icarus in the Pennines | MICHELLE D'SOUZA

These hills are heredity, so, I follow one of two paths
my father taught me, the river, dark as peat and destiny.
Some folk would pay for the view from our prison,
over steeply woven hills, castle crags, refurbished mills.
We're neither strangers to exile nor partial to routine
with a shared love of cloud collages and ornithology.
Am I the victim of his cleverness, his deportations?
Those candled, diligent hours he spent were not in vain.
We will never tire of quarrelling over ethics or design –
Yesterday, I spent £5 for a silk scarf at the charity shop
No washing machine or hairdryer in the studio exposed
a dash of my hubris, a southern capitalist limiting costs.
Only the birds hope despite the sun's incremental leave.
They slant across the morning's congealed skies like
brushstrokes, and from the river's belly the risen song
of Emily Brontë's 'necessary' stones atones the ego
as it drops, shattering the frozen pond of love's bondage.

Icing | D.J. HUPPATZ

It rose and rose and rested, cracked and cooled.
Then came the sinking: a grammatical collapse,
showers of pixels, a rainbow of fairy sprinkles.

A rise is a rise is a rise as Aunt Gertie used to
say. She didn't realise her diminishing cool-
ness quota was to blame for this satin glaze.

Restless children hold out flat cloud plates.
A swan whispers lyrics in Taylor Swift's ear.

Icing causes lesions in fish brains but high
gloss strawberry stops the scroll, freezes an
acute clog of poetry into tasty hailstones.

When cygnets shake their fluffy feathers
haters will fall into a haunted panopticon.
They lick it up, lap at it until it fills a lack.

Then endlessness begins and Uncle Charlie
teaches the children how to skin a hot dog.

They swill linguini dipped in liquid silver,
meatballs gelatinous with an algae topping
and washed down with neon blue slurpees.

Buttons unclicked, the lucky ones become
initatiates of the oven mysteries. The others
pick crumbs from the rug, wait for the melt.

Dust motes float, oblivous to their singularity.
Not even electric lime icing can save the day.

i.

no one would be as fluent as us / swimmers. gliding through what we
know as air, density augmented. our shoulders feel / brunt of gym
tiles Dad and i flipped / onto faded patchwork carpet. i still remember
/ miniature brick pattern of black and grey. now hidden beneath those
tiles / does our presence haunt them, woven as it is / in those threads?
does our sweat still simmer / underneath those rubber squares? our
backs still feel / blistered sky warming our ache.

ii.

sweat used to smell like chlorine to me. tears used to taste of it, too
/ Dad's back still aches with sudden weightlessness / redundant, his
shoulders, too / been months since he hunched / over a desk. since
he left soaked shoes on pool deck by the office door. now i return to
earn / money he no longer can / and i find everything still as we left
it: stretch cords limp on their hooks / dried blood stains just out of /
water's reach. crack in the tiles where / pool cover roller toppled over.
where Dad's ache first pooled.

iii.

here is where his back cracked like the spine of a book / here is where
i learn a new language. if movement was that language / no one
would be as fluent as us / country hoppers, us / page flickers, us / pen
wielders, us / keyboard masters, us. tab and tab and / lines lap against
the paper like pool water against the cracks.

'i see a photo…' (from rock flight*)* | *HASIB HOURANI*

i see a photo of a great heron eating a rat head-first. it's nine in the
morning a film of mucus doming my fried egg and i feel sick like i
am going to vomit. now it is on my tongue now it is caught between
molars chewing swallowing swallow sinking into gut pit.

dirty water of the aqueduct
near my house it collects the downpour
              it walks me down
the citylink
              funnelling downward downhill
waterlog the cement throat
vomit into the stream

eat a date
keep the stone
put it in your pocket

in the olden days the arab sailors were the only sailors who did not
contract scurvy while at sea they were still getting vitamin c from the
dates they packed. i do not fact check this because i trust my dad.[8]

if you are on your deathbed lying on the sand, plant a date before your
last breath and you will go straight to heaven١*. i do not fact check
this because my teacher scares me.

---

8. jeanine reads my manuscript in draft form to check the political messaging and
     highlights the word "dad" and comments "pretty sure i told him that story"

١* anas ibn malik reports that rasool allah pbuh said, *even if the resurrection were established upon one of you while he has in his hand a sapling, let him plant it.*[9]

وَأَرْسَلَ عَلَيْهِمْ طَيْرًا أَبَابِيلَ

and	he	delivers	unto	them	birds	in	flocks
	god	issues	to		aves		droves
		orders	onto				masses
		dispatches	upon				clusters
		sends					hoards

تَرْمِيهِم بِحِجَارَةٍ مِّن سِجِّيلٍ

throwing	at	them	stones	of	clay
casting			rocks	from	
launching					
shooting					
flinging					
slinging					

i am walking down the street and there is a rock on the pavement and look another one. the first city i see when i see palestine is jericho. we are driving down a flat wide road in a straight line, boulders and hollows on either side and i'm thinking *yes i made it* and then *yes i get it now* because it is about the earth. it has always been about the earth.

---

9. "Hadith on Trees," Daily Hadith Online The Teachings of Prophet Muhammad, accessed November 2022, https://www.abuaminaelias.com/dailyhadithonline/2012/11/24/plant- tree-ressurection/.

the jewish ethnostate was thought up by someone else
the french and the british
1799[10] one hundred years
before zionism two hundred years
before ███████████████████████

13. did you have a rock in your pocket?
    a. yes
        i. did you throw it?
            ١. yes
                ١. with the intent to seriously harm?
                    a. yes
                        i. twenty years away
                    b. no
                        i. ten years away
            ٢. no
    b. no

it's not enough
it won't do
we can't only choke
back the state that chokes us when
      the state that chokes us
is being breathed alive
      by bigger empires

---

10. Abdul Wahhab Al Kayyali, *Zionism Imperialism and Racism* "The Historial Roots of the Imperialist-Zionist Alliance" (London: Croom Helm, 1979) 9–24.

empires that created
the state that chokes us
to keep the empires
empires

god created the earth and said *gibril go plant these stones all over it* and
gibril took them and because we live on a sphere the rocks spread
like butter: evenly, melting. and then gibril tripped on the taut string
border into palestine and his bag of rocks spilled and now our country
is a monument of stones, and a garden of stones, and a reminder of *do
not fall over.* a reminder of *when you are fleeing, look to your feet.*

eat a date keep the stone
in your pocket: the weight of the afterlife
of ammunition

a rock isn't a rock

until it is thrown

and then it is a weapon

and then you are put into a box

what a throat
on that waterbird
to eat a rat whole

I see you I will never let you go | NATALIE HARKIN

APB Special Aptitude. General Remarks: You are aged between 11 and 15 / allocated work options and your aptitude ranked / you are on their record and they say … you are 'Quiet, reliable, with colourless personality' / you are 'Not very intelligent, rather colourless, but suited to domestic service, willing' / you are 'Cheerful and bright, somewhat erratic, willing but slap-dash' / you are 'Active, quick, assertive, morose at times, out of school behaviour questionable' / you are 'Quiet demeanour, resents correction' / you are 'Below average intelligence, simple giggling type, inclined to foolish behaviour' / you are 'Bright, quick bird-like, full of initiative but dishonest' / you are 'Undersized, bright nature with little ability' / you are 'Nervous and resents correction, easily abashed, sulks' / you are 'Good girl, average ability, needs encouragement' / you are 'Backward, fat, lazy, careless' / you are 'Low intelligence, ineffectual, ungraceful' / you are 'Willing, quick worker, good housemaid type' / you are 'Rather unstable, sulks but quick and active' / you are 'Clean and tidy, rather conceited, work and behaviour satisfactory' / they say… they say… they say you are.[1]

I see you. I'm listening: You are all ages / your blood-memory your record and I say … you are Narungga rockpool sea-star and hot-pink sunset skies / you are Kaurna soaring ibis mangrove salt-marsh gentle tides / you are Kokatha fresh waterhole bush-plum translucent-shale / you are Mirning cliff-headlands shifting sand-dune singing whale / you are Adnyamathanha sandstone ochre-cave and canyon's peak / you are Nukunu light-sharded valley mighty river-red-gum creek / you are Barngarla salt-bush and pink-lake horizon shimmer / you are Yankunytjatjara spinifex rainbow-rock and purple-flower / you are Ramindjeri stringy-bark casuarina pink-gum shelter / you are Nauo emu-bush oyster-bed crystal water / you are Ngarrindjeri fresh lagoon cockle-midden river's mouth / you are Wirangu star-light and desert sea-cliff gathering cloud / you are Peramangk dense bushland winding-ridge to mallee-plain / you are Arabunna gibber-rock desert-pea and rising mound-spring steam / you are Boandik limestone-breeze caves volcanic-blue deep as night / you are Ngadjuri rolling range and escarpment's first-light / you are sovereign you are radiant you are songline you are love / you are … all of this, so much more , and none of their above.

---

1. GRG 52/1/0/47/1938/PP. 27-37: Assessment of children at Point Pearce and Point McLeay.

January: Variations on Sadness | MARJON MOSSAMMAPARAST

after Magritte

There is no sadness,
not in the egg, not in the chicken,
not in whichever came first.
The freshly lain
are destined to be hard-boiled
and contemplated, at a distance
up close, by their kin.
A mother studying the child
foretells, pluck by pluck,
her own bare body: you have seen it,
white-raw on your board,
you have opened your mouth
in philosophy.

That morning I stood in the sea,
a surprised prophet tipped
with newly-gathered visions
through a prism of light.
Holidaying families, my good friend,
the banal heaving lighthouse
all spake of January's two-headed god:
you have walked too,
between beginning and end
back towards inheritance
seen and been seen, consummated

and the old world, despite rapture,
against argument,

cycles again on itself
getting and begetting,
shivering, mewling, spry.

Note: This poem references René Magritte's painting *A Variation on Sadness* (1957)

Jina Yanmanha – walking
| *CHARMAINE PAPERTALK GREEN*

    Wanarayimanha – colonial way!
Jina yanmanha *into the mindset of the Midwest*
I see a lot of sheep sipping their teas or beers
Walking to the beat of Pauline and Peter like zombies
Strutting to the tunes of racism, prejudice and bigotry
They walk around a lot on social media with their fingers
Frothing hate and an imagined fear from their minds
    Wanarayimanha – on Country way!
Jina yanmanha *on Country eases this colonial madness*
She talks in a way that calms the spirit and the racing mind
She offers gifts of bush foods and carpets of wildflowers
Country is the healing blanket ready to receive and give
The sound of her running waters or lapping waves offers
A natural medicine that cannot be replicated in a chemist
    Wanarayimanha – what that way!
Jina yanmanha *and being pushed into a 26th January fight*
The white, blue and red sequin dresses and Utes driving
Along Marine Terrace with large flags like an accident
Waiting to happen whilst all the walkers stroll along
The foreshore footpath eager for the firework sky gift
Sure, we want to celebrate but not on that date thanks!
    Jina yanmanha
    Jina yanmanha
    Jina yanmanha

31 January 2025

Note: In Wajarri 'Wanarayimanha' means walking in a group, 'jina yanmanha' means walking.

I.

The perpetual rose begins as a seed asleep.

In the palace of the Babylonian king Nebuchadnezzar II, *a huge palace with terraced gardens*—the monumental edifice is irrigated by way of an ingenious mechanism, channelling running water upwards from the ground. An exercise in the reversal of gravity: in the engraving by the Dutch master, at the top right corner of the print, the gardens can be seen, suspended in slabs of thick green behind the broken obelisk and ruined city walls.

Other evidence of sumptuous gardens, in the ruins of the royal residence. These, for instance, were large grounds reserved for hunting. The king was fond of riding out, in the clear and deathless morning, to decimate his population of stags. At the height of the Persian ascension, the many wings of the palace were lavishly decorated as verdant Arcadias: gardens moving into rooms and the rooms into gardens. A perpetuum mobile, through which is fed discordant dreams.

At Granada, surviving until 1492 *as the last Moorish bastion.* Once stood a pavilion surrounded by pools. At Alcázar in Seville. At Generalife, rising fifty metres above the Alhambra, a pleasance with verdant lawns—each could be suddenly flooded, by means of a hidden system of springs.

It was then, out of the searing heat that we, chancing upon an oasis—

Bounded by a large lake. The design incorporating the new technology of optical terracing. By which the perspective of the eye is multiplied, through additional visions stacked above and below.

II.

Each walled garden has two entrances. There are no exits of which to speak.

The Old French medieval epic *Roman de la Rose*, an allegorical novel composed by two authors more than forty years apart: in which a young man, wandering lucid asleep, falls in love with a rose. Central to this genre of visionary literature, characteristic of the period, is the *visio*—the device of the dream. The thing that one might say about such works, is that *One might say that in such works time is utterly excluded from the action.*

The *Roman* sets its action in a walled garden, a *locus amoenus* with connotations of Eden, and containing the following essential elements: trees, grass, water, crystals, roses, a fountain, a mirror, time.

Time, who made our fathers old, who ages kings and emperors and will age us all.

The exterior of the garden, over which the sun shines eternally, is revealed to be Hell itself, while the interior is unstable and illusory. At the bottom of the fountain the dreamer sees two prismatic crystals, which between them reflect the image of the garden entire. And through the *perilous mirror*: the beloved rose.

Known pests and diseases afflicting the genus *rosa*: aphids, scale, wilt, black spot, die-back, sin. *From his slack hand the garland wreathed for Eve / Down dropped, and all the faded roses shed.*

To bud a rose, one must first select a briar. Then cut out the eyes.

III.

The dream is always a scene within another dream.

These images recur on the frescoes of Pompeii, in the palace of Knossos. In *the place called the Garden of Midas, where roses grow wild.*

The Egyptian garden in the era of the New Kingdom, following the unstable Second Intermediary Period and lasting approximately five centuries, was believed to be: *a kind of intermediate zone linking this world with the next.* An immense complex divided into distinct temporal zones, the most magnificent of these was dedicated to Aton, god of the sun.

In 1661, Louis XIV, who through his long reign styles himself the Sun King, begins an extensive development of the palace and park at the hunting lodge known as Versailles. The castle is the central point from which all alleys radiate. Each section of the garden in turn branches and descends, thereby defining more and more sections

to create an extraordinary effect
as if he is floating above the earth

The world, from this perspective, appears as an ordered space, speared with light. At the centre of the rotating sphere—

Walking through the Hall of Mirrors and out of the palace—

One comes to the once-famed Pool of Apollo, buried and lost in the maze.

What is felt by visitors—at the borders of the cropped box hedges, around the ordered colonnades—is *a feeling for the end of an epoch,* its *manifold contradictions.*

IV.

First appearing in Venice at the close of the fifteenth century, the *Hypnerotomachia Poliphili* of Frances Colonna exerted a key influence on the master gardeners of the Renaissance. The author being *a monk, a prince, an authorial collective*. Or none of the above. The book details a dream journey to the garden island of Cythera, a temperate paradise comprised of innumerable interwoven labyrinths. Beyond the endless array of pergolas, arcades, and rotundas, embedded in parterres of cypresses, cedars, climbing jasmine and roses, one finds, variously arranged: the Patio de los Leones, the Patio de los Arrayanes, the Cour de la Fontaine, the Cour du Phénix.

The courtyard is designed in the shape of a cross, consistent with the received Christian Roman-Hellenic tradition: four equal squares anchored by a central fountain. Each part is cut by a channel, symbolising the four rivers of Paradise: water, sourced from nearby mountains, first passes through a series of illusory pools and cascades.

At the conclusion of the sequence, beyond the edge of the dream, lies the tomb of the lover:

The beautiful flower, who for all Poliphilo's tears cannot revive in this arid place. But if you would see me in flower, a rare picture:

With what joy did I attend the dawn, its pale rose spread into the clear and depthless sky.

It seemed to me that I slept again

Then I entered into the garden

V.

Notes:

Italicised phrases are quotes, with some amendments, from the following sources:

Mikhail Bakhtin, *The Dialogic Imagination*, edited and translated by Caryl Emerson and Michael Holquist (University of Texas Press, 1981).

Frances Colonna, *Hypnerotomachia Poliphili* (*The Strife of Love in a Dream*), translated by Joscelyn Godwin (Thames & Hudson, 2005).

Herodotus, *The Histories*, translated by Aubrey de Sélincourt (Penguin, 2003).

Ehrenfried Kluckert, *European Garden Design: From Classical Antiquity to the Present Day* (Könemann, 2005).

Guillaume de Lorris and Jean de Meun, *Roman de la Rose* (*The Romance of the Rose*), translated by Charles Dahlberg (Princeton University Press, 1995).

John Milton, *Paradise Lost* (Oxford University Press, 2004).

Love Poem with Apologies for My Genocide Grief
| *SARA M SALEH*

after Ada Limón

I think you got the worst
of me. The hours I could not
eat, scrolling through rubble and
funeral, hundreds of names
lodged behind my teeth. The way
I fell silent mid-sentence, stared blankly
past your face into a sky I don't trust
anymore.

I'd like to say this meant I felt
safe with you, the glowing phone
screen, the kuffiyeh draped over
the hallway coatrack, the words I could
not make small enough to say aloud.
But it was never that simple.

Grief is a terrible resident, settles
into your fault lines, leaves you on the
kitchen floor at 3 a.m., abandons your God,
your plans to build a family. You still
held me when I turned away,
when I recited facts like prayers:
"Four children an hour." "Starvation as a weapon."
"Entire families wiped off the register."

I'm sorry you saw me like that
jaw clenched, always braced,
emotionally depleted.
But when you said you loved me
a genocide streaming
in the background …
for maybe a little while
I convinced myself,
we, too, might survive this.

Maybe If I Keep Having A Good Time All The Time
All My Problems Will Just Go Away | LUCY VAN

Call up the ground to me feet
Lord forgive me I have lived in Melbourne

Cars are dancing
This translation is my retail prayer

**

Form is the sound of a photograph. It sounds off, sounds away, sounds like paradox, sounds like influence. It sounds like time, which is made of wood, related to techniques of cabinetmaking. I myself have been found guilty of cabinetmaking, usurping machines of precision. The very thing (sad). Or else I am guilty of shipbuilding. The very (sad) thing. The (very) (sad) (thing). The very sad (not sad) thing of the living sound of wood.

Form is costly. This is why one is generally concerned with the protagonist and the plot. The maintenance of the subplot and the background is so costly.

One is generally concerned with the protagonist. One is she. She serves the free wine at the bar and takes the photographs.

This is the subplot. It occurs twice. You will not be required to pay attention. The source of its strength is its homogeneity.

**

What did you wish upon that star?

**

Montgomery Clift sits in a wooden boat in a courtroom in upstate New York. He is sitting here because he caused an accident in a movie, *A Place in the Sun*. *What did you wish upon that star?* asks Shelly Winters, right before the accident. What did you wish upon that star, asks the district attorney, prosecuting the charge of murder of a wobbling Shelly Winters, pregnant, about to ferry at least one soul from one bank to another, asking Montgomery Clift to row the boat to the centre of the lake.

I ferry between *A Place in the Sun* and *Freud*, a movie about the career of Sigmund Freud, who was a doctor from Vienna. John Huston, who was a filmmaker from America, made the film in 1962. J-P Sartre, who was a writer from France, had his name removed from the list of contributing writers. I should have said, earlier, that Montgomery Clift was an actor from America, like John Huston. From Nebraska, like Marlon Brando. This is all from the subplot.

Freud has become interested in hypnosis. Why don't you ever hypnotise me, I ask my doctor, staring at his Roman candle, becoming interested.

We crawl out of the water and we crawl back in.

That I relate to Montgomery Clift goes without saying, though it seems I am saying it, explicitly, saying without going, the former *gamine* (*gay man, why do you think it's so confusing when we hang out together*), the gay man who is being confusing with Shelly Winters (*I will definitely marry you on the public holiday next week, don't even worry about it, baby*) while staying at Elizabeth Taylor's house right by Loon Lake. He is engulfed by her face, and this is the same face as my mother's face. *You are a young Elizabeth Taylor*, we think. He is thinking: maybe if I keep having a good time all the time all my problems will just go away. Monty, you're so mysterious, it's like you're not even here. There. Someone takes a photograph.

Montgomery Clift crawls out of the water at Loon Lake in *A Place in the Sun* and crawls into a lecture hall in Vienna. Crawls into a Paris metro station called *Freud*. Somewhere above, someone stares at a Roman candle.

Montgomery Clift plays Freud in the John Huston movie. Monty is now an expert in hysteria, an expert of the immobility on the left side of the face. He gives us Freud in the Viennese hospital. His patient takes off his shirt. His patient sits on the floor. His patient begins rowing a boat. His eyes stay closed.

You row to the middle of the lake. What happens there?
I stand up
Yes
The boat rocks
Yes
I'm falling
Yes
The boat turns over
Yes
My brother calls for help
Yes
I swim round the boat but I can't find him
Where is he
Drowned
Yes
I swim around
Yes
I swim to shore

We crawl out of the water and we crawl back in.

Form is costly. Ask Truman Capote, who dragged his publisher over a couple of decades only to leave the cunty little chapters of *Answered Prayers* when he ferried out to the other bank:

> ". . . He's so beautiful," murmured Miss Parker. "Sensitive. So finely made. The most beautiful young man I've ever seen. What a pity he's a cocksucker." Then, sweetly, wide-eyed with little girl naïveté, she said: "Oh. Oh dear. Have I said something wrong? I mean, he is a cocksucker, isn't he, Tallulah?" Miss Bankhead said: "Well, d-d-darling, I r-r-really wouldn't know. He's never sucked my cock."

He never sucked my cock, either. And that is the saddest sentence I'll ever write.

**

After I stop talking to Ruth I stop writing. I sort of just sit around watching Montgomery Clift movies. They run in a non-metaphorical sense right under me, or I ferry between them (and I think he killed Shelly Winters in *A Place in the Sun*, and I think I killed Ruth every time I pass Darebin Road on a sunny Melbourne day, or it was an accident that I caused)

They push a boat right into the courtroom. We crawl out of the water and we crawl back in—

Now, Montgomery Clift, I want you to step right into the boat and show the jury exactly what happened when the boat overturned. Take the same position you had at the time of the drowning.

You rowed to the middle of the lake
What happens then
I stand up
Yes
The boat rocks
Yes
I'm falling
Yes
The boat turns over
Shelly Winters calls out for help
I swim round the boat but I can't find her

How far apart were you when you came up?
How far exactly? From there to the jury box?
Why couldn't you swim toward her?

*

Why couldn't you swim toward her? No one is very interested in the answer, least of all Montgomery Clift, who is now receiving his final visit from Elizabeth Taylor. They're gonna give you the chair, Monty. Her face engulfs the final visit. Now this is a face. What even is a face? What happened to Monty's face? Why did Montgomery Clift enact two identical boating accidents in these movies shot more than a decade apart? Well it seems uncanny, Freud shrugs. But what's going on with you?

Why couldn't you swim toward her? Was it because the scene was so costly? Was it form? Was it form, so costly? Subplot, so costly, background so costly? Maintenance? My visible hand. My visible hand on the wood makes a sad sound; I'm afraid I'll make a sad sound. It will be so loud, so costly, the form of it, when drunk, medicated, uninsurable, two front teeth lodged in the back of my throat, sucking my own cock, I will swim toward her—

Strange light seeps through the window
dragging salt in with it. She is limpid too,
shadowing herself. Memory of the body
falling over floorboards

dragging salt in with it. She is limpid too,
vapour condensing to cloud.
Falling over floorboards—
pastel, strato, close as skin.

Vapour condensing to cloud,
stretched warning across sky.
Pastel, strato, close as skin—
too much ocean to fit in.

Stretched warning across sky,
she rattles like a stone. Time's tooth
too much ocean to fit in.
Sinking requires effort.

She rattles like a stone. Time's tooth
bites into an empty phone booth.
Sinking requires effort,
speech requires effort.

Bite into an empty phone booth.
Undrowned, she steps from the ocean.
Speech requires effort.
This room littered with memory.

Undrowned, she steps from the ocean.
Cups and bowls, cracked bodies—
this room littered with memory,
cast into slip. Feast and inventory.

Cups and bowls, cracked bodies.
How strange it is to have one,
cast into slip. Feast and inventory,
morning's mirror clean as a knife.

How strange it is to have one,
dragging salt in with it.
Shadowing herself, memory of the body.
Strange light seeps through the window.

Monostich X: Glimpses | AMANDA ANASTASI

The phone holds the man.

Art needs at least a small death.

Some goodbyes are a greeting to oneself.

I place a foot on shell-less ground.

There is a time for dropping calculations.

In the rubble, a swing set.

Keep your cards flying from your chest.

I do not accept your politeness.

I am not shivering from cold.

Now raising children as a lifestyle
we look so much like American poets,
except they had more Dexedrine
and less automation.
Amazon, for example,
brings Richard Brautigan to my door.
I tell them both to leave;
I had ordered Tom Raworth in a sling.
What did it mean to dally in Denver anyway?
I hear they never even spent
their winnings. Imagine spending them.
Not a lottery ticket in Hell did they buy.
O the boredom of a true story.
As it is, useless Americanisms
tarnish one's spectacular name.
What nationality is best appropriated
to naturalise this saturnine but saturnalian turn?
Good luck. You wait in line.
The West is in every state of exit.
'We' are boarding the rocket ship, as a family no less!

My Boyfriend, Rasputin | KERRY GREER

My boyfriend, Rasputin, watches me with eyes blue as
monkshood steeped to brew a poison tea.

My boyfriend, Rasputin, wants to marry me, kiss me, kill me.
But not in that order, not like the game.

When we have a disagreement, my boyfriend, Rasputin,
tells me to: *Lower your voice. Lower. Your. Voice.*
And I do until I'm breathing quietly,
and listening.

My boyfriend, Rasputin, studied Russian history.
He teaches French to public high school students.
He buys coffee on the way to work
in a pressed blue shirt and double-pleat pants.
He stops by the same café every day,
and when he arrives the barista
shouts, 'Hey!' like my boyfriend is a normal person,
someone you'd be happy to see at a moment's notice.
He doesn't have to say what he wants to order.
It arrives in his hands.

The wind comes in at night
from the steppes
and blows me   this way
                                        that way
                    away
the white sheet of me   filters
to the floor, where I lie flat, able to fit
under doors.

My boyfriend, Rasputin, makes me chamomile tea
and insists I drink it. He watches over me,
then carries my mug to the sink,
where he washes the dishes and studies my calendar.
Later in the week, he asks if I made it to the doctor,
if I got my assignment in on time. He knows where
I will be before I make it there, if I'm running late,
and he knows made-up appointments I add to my calendar
purely for his sake, so he can imagine
I'm really good at doing what he likes
when he imagines me living my real life
away from him all day.

If my boyfriend, Rasputin, visits me after work,
he's in shirtsleeves and suede shoes.
I see his hands, his wrists
thick from days in the field
of the mind.
His belt buckle shines
in the afternoon sun.

Little Flower, Little Petal, my Love,
my boyfriend, Rasputin, says to me.
Where were you today?
I waited for you in your driveway
with fruit and cake and wine
to share, to celebrate. And now again,
you keep me waiting at your door
before you let me enter your house.
You wouldn't have another man here, would you?

he jokes, his eyes flicking like a pocket-knife
at the threshold of my bedroom.
My Love, my Jo, my Little Rose, he says,
feigning a Scottish brogue like Burns or maybe
someone he knows. *You are alone, I see.*
He laughs, flashing just the edges of his teeth.
I exhale relief, doubting my sanity,
my ability to hide a whole human
beside my bed and remember doing so.
Underneath the joke, a seam of love
running dark and ancient as coal
in a black and holy cave.
How can I see in?
How can I see out?

If my boyfriend, Rasputin, is the colour blue—
petals streaming across a path in the early autumn wind—
I am red and white, trail of a limping animal
in the snow. He has known me
since girlhood, which means
I knew him
when he was a boy, and smaller and softer,
with the same eyes watching.

As in any perfect system, decay grows from the centre.
By which I mean: me.
As in any fairytale, the real reason love continues
can only be hinted at.

When he can't sleep, my boyfriend, Rasputin,
bakes me black bread and honey-glazed biscuits.
He brings them to my door in the morning,
kissing the top of my head. Other nights,
he parks outside my window, to argue with me
on the phone where he can see me. If I creep
like a ghost in my own home to the curtains
to close them, he is suddenly at the door
in a rage. *It's not what you did*, he says.
It's that I couldn't see you doing it.

At first, the handle.
       At last, the lock.
   The line he crosses—
metal turning, turning until it stops.
And my hand on the key, and my voice speaking,
low and soft and slow: *Sorry.*
To keep him quiet. *Come inside.* To make him leave
more quickly.

My mother says, *Tell me where he lives?*
What is the number plate on his car?
My boyfriend, Rasputin, lives
with his parents, but I cannot tell her this.
She will find him, will knock at his door,
will meet with his mother, and we'll be children again,
hiding in the woods before the snow comes.
In the white morning, there will be no trace of us,
no path to follow home when I come to my senses.

The fields of light will touch me everywhere
sharply as I walk a little behind
that man, falling into his footprints.
My mother says, *I bet he parks outside.*
What car does he drive? I will find him,
I will tell him he must leave you alone.
How she knows, she knows.

I tell my boyfriend, Rasputin, that the moon is rose-
gold tonight, the edges of it shimmering
in the shadow cast by the earth. *A Worm Moon,*
I say. He asks how I know this—
What time were you outside tonight, and why?
He wants the facts, not the moon,
the silly woman's eyes looking up at it,
watching how slowly,
slowly, carefully it pulls away from the earth
over time.

My boyfriend, Rasputin, looks after everything
he owns. When he takes off his belt, he coils
the leather like a snake around his hand
then sets it on my dressing table,
holding the buckle steady
so the strap doesn't unravel.
I know he's not going anywhere.

Night vision: apology to a late-diagnosed daughter
Autism | ESTHER OTTAWAY

for jamming the toothbrush into your mouth while you cried and fought your body being entered for setting you up to fail with reward charts you could only manage for a day for scolding and enforcing consequences for denying you pocket money trying to make you do chores you could never do and didn't understand for forcing food between your lips and frightening you into swallowing for the calm lengthy reasoning I did with you as to why you should do better for feeling choked that you needed every inch of my personal space all the time for praising you when you'd done something right when praise just made you more anxious for towering over your tiny body and pointing my finger as I shouted for not realising after you'd gotten off a chair thirty times and I'd put you back on thirty times that there was a learning problem not a discipline one for bellowing at you to go to sleep sleep sleep for putting you back in your bed over and over like Supernanny said until you were beside yourself and so was I for denying you screen time which made you start peeling skin off yourself in agitation for pushing you into the bath and out of the bath and telling you to stop whingeing as I did your hair with the brush you howled was sharp and the hairdryer you howled was loud for putting back on you the clothes and shoes you perpetually pulled off for losing sympathy about your endless injuries for never telling my friends that you bit your mouth till it bled and wiped the blood on the walls and that your ceaseless anxiety had worn you to a bag of bones and that I walked on eggshells instead of enjoying my parenting for leaving you wailing in time-out for anything I did to you to assuage my own distress for being a new parent who had no language for what you were, for being slow to see you, I'm sorry. You are parallax, shoal, diaspora. You are percipience, cloud-measurer, reverie. You are love-scar, bioluminescence.

October 13th | RACHEL WHITE

Bark shed, the redgum
stands near a stone—
makeshift grave.
Radio drones: hostages
in Gaza; we voted down
The Voice. Blade of knife
in avocado seed, its shape
exacts a hole in the flesh.
Melamine environs
alchemized by a girl's
cobalt brushstroke,
its blue pigment bleeding
into a paler version of
itself. Emerging hydrangea
heckled by body-shaming
rape joke boy who
points a choking finger:
"You're targeting me!"
Crash of security door
shudders. We take one
collective breath. Read
judgement of Solomon,
concept of tearing
a baby in two to prove
a point. My son rhymes
'grief' with 'leaf'
in a word game. Funny
how it keeps shaking off
the tree like autumn rust.
No velvet ears to knead
or kisses to comfort
in this house of sticks.

I read Glück died. Repeat
the route from pet hospital
to home, barbed seeds of
plane trees flank the road.

Open the frog app. This is an app for collecting facts.
Record and upload. A singer's added to the frog song map.
The frog app is a translation app. I record clapsticks
and duelling washboards. I record a zydeco band.
Common eastern froglet is what the Australian Museum sends back.
Thank you for being part of our census. Why not join us on earbud safari?
The *green stream frog* shrugs its styrofoam package;
the *southern barred frog* shells peas in a box made of timber
the *striped marsh* is chopping; this fretsaw work is the *wallum rocket*;
the *broad-palmed frog* thumbs a comb nonchalant
as the *eastern banjo* who's floating up lobs.
I once asked, like a fool, where the tennis club was.
But with the frog app I found acceptance, found the guide
who leads me from avant garde throat singers, hiccupping buddhas,
back to the science of relative spawn depths, months for mating,
species distribution maps. Getting up close
the frog tells me whose pupils are vertical, round or flat
and bears unflinching witness to blemishes, spots and bands.
The frog app will not curate online personae.
Its expert identifications are cleansing a twittersphere
shouting alternative facts. For civil and well-informed discourse
open the frog app. Top up your swamp. Replenish the tank.

Other Eminent Hands | JOHN KINSELLA

And as five zones th' aetherial regions bind,
Five, correspondent, are to Earth assign'd:
The sun with rays, directly darting down,
Fires all beneath, and fries the middle zone:
The two beneath the distant poles, complain
Of endless winter, and perpetual rain.
Betwixt th' extreams, two happier climates hold
The temper that partakes of hot, and cold.

—OVID VIA JOHN DRYDEN*

It's a mantra, isn't it? Now a gifting
of the driest six months here in 150 years —
            'since records began',
            which the panting
wagtail calls a grotesque expression.
Change is many of us working hand
            over hand, making
            stands or semi-forgetting.
We've arrived from a wet zone wetter
than usual, and this is the drift. Creation
            swelling or cracking
            in every realm. Remember
the funnels collecting smutty rain,
the swaying of tall trees till they split.
            And now any roots
            unable to reach below
the outer shell withering in the dark,
or lit up when those cracks reach down.
            Either way. Eventually,
            we'll rid language of words

---

* from *Metamorphoses* 'translated into English verse under the direction of Sir Samuel
  Garth by John Dryden, Alexander Pope, Joseph Addison, William Congreve and
  other eminent hands' [https://knarf.english.upenn.edu/EtAlia/ovidmeta.html]

of change or words of weather, we'll
acclimatise to whatever binds lives
	from end to end.
	Other eminent hands
will pretend translation when they
are remaking in own images. An
	Easter Monday
	and the road toll rises.
An Easter Monday and blue trees wilt.
A woman asleep or collapsed on the street
	of a country town
	stares horizontal
towards the railway line and its post-
flood traffic of intercontinental supplies.
	In this small town are 26 people
	homeless... and counting.
Other people are enjoying the holiday —
an easy day-trip from the city. It's hot
	but not chronically hot
	as it has been. This new
beginning. This continuation. The river
cradle forgetting what it can hold,
	and their eminences
	searching out a word
that incorporates 'sun', 'solipsistic', 'profit',
'prophet', 'business', 'rain', 'dryness', and love.

Otopos | DOMINIQUE HECQ

A person is a community of beings,
an 'us' as much as an 'I'

— JANE HIRSHFIELD

1.

Lulled by the night's lingering breath, the city hibernates. Funnelling wind at your back, you skirt the creek. Follow the trickle of bruises the light leaves in its wake. You take the path down to the bridge, the no-sun enfolded in fog. Eucalypts rustle. Reeds rumour. Australian wood ducks, chestnut teals and a lone hardhead on corrugated water. Magpie larks chatter in a she-oak. A nankeen night heron darts in your path as if to say you don't exist. Under the bridge, a black swan on a nest intermeshed with plastic. Now the wind embraces you. Mud sucks at your boots—*ssk ssk ssk*. Rainbow lorikeets, fairy corellas and musk lorikeets clatter about. You climb the escarpment. Here, creeping bent grass, English broom, arum lily, prickly pear, periwinkle overflow garden fences. Gusts of wind through veils of bridal creeper and poison ivy.

2.

Walk with me, says the voice drowning in its own rasping sound. You become it, the voice, a shapeshifter like the creek itself, brimming with unspoken thoughts, voiceless bubbles, breathless refuse.

Waterfall. Murky calm where the path tilts and narrows.

Here, the water curves and swerves in its owns bed, pulls at silt. The current pushes it out unseen, against the sunken stepping stones.

Here, the water swirls, froths, falls and rushes towards the edge land of daydream. Towards the immargination of the page.

3.

A wattlebird babbles on the other side of the window. I replenish the water bowl. Spot a honey eater hopping about in the fuchsia.

My hand yawns. It is a beak opening.

Water breaking at the touch of a feather.

I am a magpie. Warble a wattlebird prattle.

I feel for the shape of a poem.

I live and work on the land of the Wurundjeri people of the Kulin Nation, the sovereignty of which was never ceded. I acknowledge its traditional custodians, offering respect and gratitude to their ancestors, elders and families past, present and in perpetuity.

Australia always was and always will be, Aboriginal land.

I feel shame, not quite guilt, for knowing so little about the languages, cultures, and customs of the Kulin Nation. For purloining the bird's call. For naming it *prattle*.

(*To unwrite the I from the poem. Think of it.*)

4.

Words are possums crawling up the walls of silence. They have razor-sharp claws. They pounce. They can see in the dark. They will poke the apple of your eye. Hook your mouth shut. Rip you to shreds. Tear up your dreams one letter at a time.

Pause.

Consider the damage to the root of your tongue.

Don't worry: they will burst the blisters tenderly. At dawn they'll scuttle around the idea of noise. Then they will burrow under the vault of your ribs and nibble at the chambers of your heart.

Here, they will persuade you to shrug off your graphomania, glossolalia, xenolalia. Tendency to anaphora and… apocrypha.

5.

Cold bites, breath dissipates
gossamer mist nudges the windowpane.

Sky low over Melbourne.

The sun wears a corona of grey that keeps it away
from the day
like a foreign body's swathing
so intimate it blinds.

I fumble for the shape of a poem.

Pelting rain. The wind dies. Ink spills.

This is how the I unwrites itself from the poem.

The sky won't fall for all its broken lights.

Waves of wheeling spectral spokes follow
you like a sailing dream.

Open the window.

Float past your life.

You could go along a straight line for light years;
the angle at which you'd see sun and moon
and shade and sea would be the same.

This is how you unwrite yourself from the poem.

A boat loaded with broken mirrors sets alight
memories of a past for live masks.

A boat loaded with dry brambles lights nightmares
of a present for death faces.

A boat loaded with paper aeroplanes matches
dreams of a future for unborn forms.

On the nearby shore, ash of us in shimmering shadows.

the summer the world turned eighteen
we drove around with a blondie cd stuck in the player
for months we learnt the rise and fall of debbie's range
that's why each sticky-thighed passenger
still knows every word to rapture
on thursdays we would shoplift in our spares
until the incident with the blue beaded purse
made our habits go underground
I tasted a cheeseburger learnt suburban rituals
wrappers strewn on the backseat with other forms of longing
tasting like the fantasy of adulthood for a dirt road kid

the summer we turned eighteen
I yearned to be yearned for
to make sense of my desire
to have a place in the constellation of someone else's trash
in those days I assumed I would die in a car
and with jittery acceleration I worried I would die a virgin
I cared deeply about that status
until it changed and there is no word for the time after
my fear shifting then to dying without ever being in love

nothing pierces a teenager like a guitar solo
between the coke bottles and chocolate wrappers
gathering under the feet of our liberation
I would go and hold her hand now
say that love will come crashing in without invitation
this road stretches all the way until it comes back again

and so perhaps that's why we drive the long way home
mouthing along to the lyrics one more time
to catch the spectre of sunset
to become the mote caught in the vanishing rays
to inhabit for a moment the possibilities that still surround us

Pantoum | STUART BARNES

for Martin Ingle

How to write
a poem
about obsessive-compulsive disorder?
Turn your back to unlocked doors

(a poem
seeks vulnerability).
Turn your back to Unlocked———doors
will kaleidoscope. Say The I

seeks vulnerability.
Speak three times of death———odd numbers
will kaleidoscope. Say The eye
will come to no harm.

Speak three times of death, odd numbers———
your sweethearts
will come to no harm.
Let the charcoal stovetop be

your sweet heart's
anchorage.
Let the charcoal stovetop be.
Polish questioning's

anchorage.
Gently revolve lines,
polish questionings
(this poem is one).

Gently revolve lines
about obsessive-compulsive disorder
(this poem is one
how-to). Write.

Poem approaching the possible | SHARI LYNELLE

It is she. It is she again. It is preference. Words in the mind on the ground speaking not writing but history in the air. Yellow. For blue. And yellow. For blue as blue speaking. The first association was arrogance. History and arrogance. Contemporaneity and oversight. Pairing of blue and yellow. Slivers of preference and literate. As written history might keep. The cool oversight whose soft leaves water. And later breaking. Slips.

—CARLA HARRYMAN

She is done with melting clocks
and abstract interiors painted by white men.
A beast or falcon's face
doubled in cloth draped over the back,
domestic. Monstrous

                        nylons and plastics
                        break down, are already breaking down
the slow melt interior
      oceans,
            rivers,
                 sand.
She *is* part river, part plastic.

She casts herself out
in spirals,
        out of the galleried picture
no matter how clitoral its delicate light.

She is done being hung
        small moments of beauty
or quartered   each to the other's emotional suns.

What she wants   is already
         breathing
the endangered   fourth tense[i]

have breathed, will breathe, am breathing
swirling its river above.

Seven days hence,
> *though smiling doesn't even occur to her*[ii]
she will speak from her bones,
> she will speak from her glands
furred and incurred, mellifluous
sixty-five thousand cerulean
subject to no man

walking from ocean
back up through river sand
back into the Yes of the breathable

humming already in language
> older than iodine
> older than canvas
older than hers alone or simple
> seawater
>> freshwater
>>> sand—

---

i. See Richard Flanagan, 'The Voice and Our Inauthentic Heart', *The Monthly*, July 2023.
ii. Clarice Lispector, 'The Waters of the World', *Complete Stories*, Penguin Random House, p.402.

Paradigm | *ALI COBBY ECKERMANN*

In the dawn she washes her hands
noticing messages inscribed on her
finger nails, petite markings of an
ancient script read when landscape
was lore, when landscape was love
in natural form. every grapheme is
an advice building to words ridged
into keratin plates etched to soothsay,
to remember the garden before our
neglect, to remind of a time when
greed was unrighteous, an epiphany
set on the nail plate, a counter force
of rebellious calligraphy that begs
to restore before death, her eyes
are drawn here, she recollects deep
love of the land, old wisdoms warn
and warn the catastrophe of greed.

poem for nina | DOMINIC SYMES

the world is bound to be unkind to you
    but your parents are not
I am not   nor are your other aunts & uncle

true too the seasons are bound to change
they *will* change
    sometimes without you knowing
while   other times
    this will be all you can be sure
       you know
(you know?)

    I'm 90 per cent convinced the night sky
isn't far away (not endless, nor expansive)
    but the roof of a child's bedroom

    nina   before you could speak
       we *held* you

I first held you last week when you were 2 days old

so if you're older & ever lost for words
    you can ask one of us who held you then
       to hold you again
          just by squeezing one of our hands

I promise to try & understand you the best I can

  ahhhh   nina
    tonight I caught the tram
  home from work
(I didn't pay)

         & jumped into a pile of leaves
      on my street
    to hear them crunch
under my feet
     this   the week of your birthday (I'm 33)

    it is scientifically true that
the natural state of everything in the universe
        is entropy   ~ everything ~
                  dissolves to chaos

  & very rarely
if you're very lucky
  you may get to experience the illusion of control

I hated bon iver the first time
your mum played me his music
but I've come around now

the first time I met your aunt gigi at a party
I spoke to her for 10 minutes
about running shoes (brooks ghost 11s)

& we didn't date for another 15 months

    life is long
& so I've learned to not put too much faith
    in first impressions

that said   I am very firm in the feeling that
   beards are gross   (imagine kissing that?)
  but I think moustaches are mysterious

charming   ticklish
     & debonair
          & this will not change
    unless your dad shaves his at your mum's stern request

    also I dry retch at the thought of eating any more
fennel or anchovies in my lifetime

& after my 24th birthday
    I vow never drink rum-based cocktails
       on a pirate-themed pancake boat (again)

that is to say – some lessons we learn very easily
       others we're doomed to repeat
         until we really learn them

full disclosure
I'm very bad at buying presents
  so sorry in advance

also   this may change

but for now

I promise I'll try harder

nina nina nina   the most important thing
           I want to tell you is
            that while I have spent a lot of my life
        feeling unworthy of love
         witnessing the way
       that in the first few days   you were alive

people *loved* you

(& this before you could even *open your eyes*
let alone recite times tables
    score a hat trick in soccer
        get a perfect ATAR
            give a speech to your graduating
                year at law school)

                            reminded me
                    that everyone is ALWAYS
                    worthy of love

                            but most especially YOU

you beautiful tiny hairy baby

        call me if you ever want to know about drugs
            your parents are far too good

can I make it up the hill   how saying what you think leads to poverty   I sit
to rest among the she oaks   how violence leads to poverty how saying
what you think leads to poverty   she was underwater lying in the middle
of the road with a sheet of plastic over her head   how violence leads to
poverty how sexual assault leads to poverty   she was underwater lying in
the middle of the road with a sheet of plastic over her head   he was saying
we can walk under water through the river   how sexual assault leads to
poverty how hard physical labour leads to poverty   he was saying we can
walk under water through the river   I was standing on a half-submerged
rock   how hard physical labour leads to poverty   these trees shaded me
here before my surgery   I was standing on a half-submerged rock   how
poetry leads to hard physical labour   these trees shaded me here before
my surgery   on a full moon night when we sat at the picnic table talking
about getting back together   how poetry leads to hard physical labour
how ill health leads to poverty   on a full moon night when we sat at the
picnic table talking about getting back together   they are in flower now
how ill health leads to poverty   they were here when we ran up from our
NYE's picnic on the beach when the storm came   they are in flower now
how poverty leads to ill health   they were here when we ran up from our
NYE's picnic on the beach when the storm came   they preside here on
the eve of my birthday   how poverty leads to ill health   how poverty leads
to housing insecurity   they are here presiding on the eve of my birthday
how the assessment sits like a toad in the bottom of the well   how poverty
leads to housing insecurity   how poverty leads to violence   how the
assessment sits like a toad in the bottom of the well   every tree a church
how poverty leads to violence   how poverty leads to the loan to value
ratio   every tree a church   I sit among the she oaks   how poverty leads
to the loan to value ratio   and the hill

Queen Tide | CHRIS ANDREWS

Silver all irretrievably strewn:
one night the sky-safe blew.

Eel-like a dark line swims from the past:
last week the drowned bell tolled.

Until it comes up nobody knows
how far the blind mole fared.

Haunted oblivious millions live
along a long-stuck fault.

I put it out there and let it go:
a mandarin moon rose.

A queen tide comes for the tillerman.
Tonight the fire-owl flies.

There's a new crack in the pedestal.
Well sapped, unsighted mole.

Where was it hidden, this daring-all?
Last night the dream-gown whirled.

Say this alliance was forged to fail.
The drunken promise holds.

I pay this line out into the dark:
last night the blind mare foaled.

i've been reading a lot but can't say what's taken up
. it's easier to track the ball when it's moving away from the camera
. company desires crude to be at once scarce and plentiful
. nodding, i can allude to capillary action, though not without wincing
. how much in a gallon? how many in a barrel? tell me of five million?
. x texts: *baby i'm in new zealand.* i can't say what's taken up

. the pressure of time folds on remnant body matter
. in search of diagnoses; a vision from little camera
. according to a man named gold it all comes from active microbes
. nodding, my saturn had returned before i ever looked it up
. while i try to hold the notion of a million orbits around the sun
. her employers split but there's an nda, she isn't going to breach it

. i text: *we need to talk about what it is we're doing*
. the man's name was gold, you cannot make this up
. while i try to hold the textures of the language used by traders
. it's difficult knowing where to start with online family members
. unleaded is less than a dollar; i have no place to be
. in this country we'll burn five hundred swimming pools every week

. olympic-sized, the room is reasonable with a south facing window
. *i'm not sure that i believed in it, even in retrospect*
. five million barrels would fill three hundred and seventeen olympic pools
. lach pauses to take a call from the boyfriend of a cheating student
. at some point we were molecules, nodding in a sea vent
. *my keyboard is broken, look,* i can't say what's taken up

. it's the may of breakups again, i laugh and chris agrees
. in search of excitement, murray buys a new drip machine
. caro's boy was going back to ireland, so they split but he got stuck
. we assume a flat rate of combustion, the whole extraction system
. in ten years since that spill, it's difficult to say what's taken up
. sometimes going online is to bruise the place you write from

. local broadcasters are celebrating the annual return of spider crabs
. liz has gotten into gardening, lucy ponders getting back to perth
. each ingredient on the list makes some promise re: its sources
. it can be hard to hold these images, this time spent apart
. *i got up this morning*, says s, *and watched the news for four hours*
. nodding, in a normal week of oil we'd use five hundred up.

Removal from Corpse | DEREK CHAN

It's fallacious to expect the dead
to be bathing in broad daylight
let alone a lifeguard to recline more
luxuriously than an archaic torso.
Today the cancer institute volunteers
ask me five questions concerning the future
of sun prevention, only to pay me
with stickers resembling a geometrically
inaccurate scarecrow. What do we mean
when we say *make room for the dead*?
Like the earth, what I want succumbs.
By the end of the calendar year,
the annual yield of nurses parachuting
into our dreams to salvage everyone
we've ever loved will be equal to the ragged
limbs of moonlight pulling out daffodils
the Spring failed to invent in time.
You weep. You rot. The relation
of the relation glimpsed only when
the brain stops. Naturally, you see god.
Naturally, a dog turns the grasses defective
and the story begins again. Over the river
is the soul and through the woods
is the body, to which we always go.
Who tosses these crumbs and who
will use them to pry open the hidden
casket of the horizon? This whole place is dark.
And only once have I walked towards
those distant angels if only to hear
lilacs shivering in the wind.

Ricochet | SUSAN FEALY

four foxes chase a calf
until its legs tip over   foxes—
they chew cow ears don't they?
he found a clutch of tags behind his shed
he said *the foxes*   cried when a deer released her fawn
behind his shed   four foxes   red fire engines.
merry christmas to you and you
let children ride high through rural streets— who calls
emergency and why   90% of infected rabbits
die   four foxes   red fire engines a howl
of sirens somewhere   he held a mouse with battered wings—
sheltered it   inside his hand   they catch
in ceiling fans   only kindness   left to do   four foxes   red
fire engines   a howl of sirens   they called her
a fucking moll   four foxes   blue tags—
red   a howl

1

a dog's endless desire for the ball

2

the morning star

3

a building under construction
loses reflected light

the diagonal stripe of a rail
crosses the balcony

4

in the park a man with rotisserie and generator
barbecues a whole pig

mangroves close-by on Powell's Creek,
ships timber in the mud

a small yellow spider
lit up in the branches

5

in the suburbs all
is conjunction
             pop radio
through undergrowth
where cats stalk each other

lorikeets, cockatoos, an insistent koel
whose red eye mines the sunset

books, objects
on the tablecloth

tallowwood, orange
at dusk,

the first hours
of daylight saving

6

a generator rumbles
as clouds build over Drummoyne

streets drain
to the Harbour,

the flat blue of Canada Bay
one edge of an island continent

7

night birds
a high-pitched twit twit
almost an insect

then sunrise through palms
idiocies of a presidential race

I liked there was a town
called Truth or Consequences
it sounded apocalyptic
but was really the name
of a quiz show

8

on Cape Solander
massed on the north of gullies,
flannel flowers, white
with pale leaves

at Kurnell, a church
on a narrow block,
its crenellated tower
bricklayer's gothic

9

Confectioners Way:
industry commemorated by street names

what else was here? a motor registry,
an art deco salesroom for luxury cars
factories and showrooms from the forties and fifties

10

Zoe's pictures, her sense of organic form
(I think of Billy Jones, his intense drawings, the focus
of the truly stoned

(I think also that I forgot
to defrost the sausages

(that's organic form for you

11

'juniper berries bloom in the heat'

12

each wrong turn
leads to another

then Chowder Bay

the waving kelp
pale blue and green

bathers dive
off the pier

the circus continues
(on Macquarie Street and Capitol Hill)

the sun dips behind elms,
rooftops of the neighbour flats

13

it's the season of mattress-dumping
it's the year of parrot fever
so why am I shaking?

Sequela | LINDSAY TUGGLE

Show me the beauty of a body contorted by thrall.
Then, show me the thrall.

Shame is a vast word.

The girl with violence in her lap
never goes astray again.

Her face,
an unstoppable fist
                    of dust.

What secret suicides her suntanned lips?
She used to run rampant in palatial halls.

In service to a master who made her over in his image,
unredeemed by vacant possession.

Heredity demands an outlier,
so she became our gaudy heretic.

In our father's house there were many rooms
            but no doors.

With each new wound we wondered
at the spellcraft of our bodies.

We are not remembering the remembering.
We are palimpsests, after all.

Memory is an inconstant bedfellow
so you must learn to make space.

Hold it loosely to avoid bloodletting.

This is the first of many tests:
Learn to sleep beside the blade.

Begin by thinking of the knife
as an extension of your hand.

Not a tool or a weapon, but another, sharper
angle of your own body.

Beauty is the work of war.
The history of gender is violence.

In both countries I have called home,
rape is now a prerequisite to governance.

It has taken me half a century to realize
The call is coming from inside the house.

shadow birds | MARK ROBERTS

look behind the lines of police
shadow birds circle the statues
they will roost tonight
tomorrow the ground
will be covered
in black feathers

Sister Cumulus | DEBBIE LIM

She arrives on a roll call of winds,
talks in billows of ever-drifting advice.
Precipitous, declares: *You are the stone*
of the family as she ripples the room:
now drizzle, now squall, scattering
a trail of ice crystals over the carpet, leaving
damp patches on the rug. But when skies
blow clear, she floats above the sill
and grades emotions by altitude:
All things, she says, *can be understood*
according to their height above sea level.
A halo-effect rises behind her head,
and I remember she is a distant relation
of the sun. Her smiles are long veils
that form low on the horizon. I move slowly
in her presence, as if over ground glass,
aware of old crevices, my glacier-like tongue.
Come nightfall, I am crouched on the floor,
watching every thin movement
at the window.

Situation Y | JELENA DINIC

Yesterday feels like it didn't happen.
The voice in your head is a day louder.

Take small breaths.
In and out.

Pause.
This is just a panic attack.

Another thought can destroy you.
What you know turns against you.

A horse deserts you on a battlefield.
Before you learn why

shake the drawers open
search for the pen as if it were the proof.

When you leave things behind
they follow you.

It hurts like a mistake.
Yours or not, it is always yours.

Believe
you are believable.

This drawer needs reorganising.
A reminder you never needed.

Pull it out. Sort your debts.
Weigh your words.

Dip into this war.
Place a full stop near a wound.

Soft Wash | AIDAN COLEMAN

Fans in the new-hatched
season, choiring your net position,
the familiar wink of your name—

your enemies: a derby.
Streamlined to blue versus green,
minus those olfactory kinks

of place—the niggle of the actual.
The flareless air
fills with paper. Heads

bobbling on a cash-breeze,
among the miscellany
of lucent memorabilia.

A gratitude that labour oils,
scratching the backs
that it airbrushes. You load

a footballer with a few ideas
that they can say back to you
with gathering conviction.

There is this spaciousness
beyond the want
of an outside.

before killing a pig, be kind, do it humanely, stick it close
to its pasture-fed heart, blood ribbons out, language ribbons in

the abattoir worker, a pork laureate, the light of the
electric stunner, a pork heaven, the poem, a pork chop

chewed close to the bone, a memory of the world's most consumed
meat, a meat as common as poetry, a thing so common that even

Gina Rinehart wrote one, in deep allegiance to mining, affixed it to
a 30-ton iron ore boulder, a poem as pointless as Google reviews of waterfalls

or celebrities returning from space & we are the only animals who 'do'
'PDFs', 'infinite scroll', 'girlbossing', 'marketing', 'humane slaughter', poetry

all different ways to touch the void, the original poem, in
different intensities & through different veils, poetry finds

its way through, the green that bursts open bitumen's weals,
let's not reinvent the ocean, says a board executive, glossolalia in

all major supermarkets & from the right angle, even a pigeon's throat
is an event of light & in this country, a fire has been burning

underground for over 6000 years, o hollowed out
earth, o so many voids, o not enough time to write them

too busy being a valued employee, too busy being a
valued customer, too busy valuing work-life-lobotomy balance

all this surplus squealing, all these heavenly shards of distraction & when
I walk around at night, all I see through open windows, is everyone just

streaming television into their eyes, is that hope or just microplastics
beating through my blood & brain & heart, corpse pose really is

quite a relaxing position to have one long ugly thought about
how there is twice as much plastic as living things in the world, the

corporate urge to laminate a burning planet, ugh the fascists
are texting me again & the bludgers that be are making an appointment to

have a meeting to develop a plan to have a meeting to discuss
a pathway to arrive at a goal, a 'goal' being the shit version of a dream

& we are making an appointment to have a meeting
to develop a plan to have a meeting to arrive at

unlimited poetry
inside us

unlimited possibility
outside us

Sous Rature in Sabah | OMAR MUSA

Supereminent, concealed, ~~the South China Sea~~ is a sentence, struck-through;
protean water god, many-faced, apophatic – ~~not China nor Philippines, not Malaysi~~
~~Vietnam, Taiwan, Indonesia, Brunei, America, Australia~~ – the voiceless voice –
eloquent, unsyllabled – shrouded in songket (dyed palsied blue & shot through
with gold) – divided, multiplying – left prone for grave robbers,

unkillable.

~~An island,~~
——— ~~blurred on a map,~~
——— ~~becomes   an air-brushed~~
——————— ~~bull's-eye.~~

Shattered surface of the sea, a fractured temporality:
        names sink, reemerge, ghostly claimants of a wereleopard's map.
Cabbage wrap an atoll in warships, salami slice island chain,
slowly silkworm-nibble, rename, take ~~legal~~ scalpel to shuddering
abdomen — UNCLOS, AUKUS — suture with invisible stitches, dissever,
stitch again, dress in grey-zone & intone the negative theology hymnal –
——— ~~not peace nor war, not peace nor war, not peace nor war.~~

~~CROSS OUT TO BRING FORWARD~~
~~CROSS OUT TO CONTEST~~
the absent presence

sail towards erasure [redacted] at the [redacted] of the [redacted],
        ~~each word a mute island if archipelago-less...~~ ———————

My nenek has never read Derrida. Never read.
Never been to a Basquiat exhibition on the HighLine.
She lives on the horizon of a Nine-Dash Line, where crabcatchers
& weaverwomen are, the hem of a plastic void, viscous, boiled to
reduction, crude oil feverdreams & eternal wayfaring of the bloodline.
Wooden stilts hold up her heart — a crab crawls down her throat —
she speaks it up in proverb. ~~Maybe I erase her even as I bring her forward,~~
    decode pantuns she never even spoke.

Wrinkled lips an asterisk* —

    ~~Can a mouth, when stitched,~~
          ~~somehow, come centre stage?~~

From Sandakan, I see islands' lambency
    but not where border starts or ceases:
I can't look back at myself from the other side:
    If I could,   I'd see a ghost struck-through.

~~* "The Sultan said that god made the earth and the sea,"~~
~~I think I heard her say. "The earth is divided amongst men. The sea is equal to all."~~

Spill | JAYA SAVIGE

Gunked in Latin, glazed in Malay,
caked in vernacular, coated in myth:
Sirenia, dugong, sea cow, mermaid.
Slick of the tongue.
                        On the whale-path

the chatty glow of algae round the hull
illuminates the scale of the spill.

He casts a caustic eye across the bloom
of lit estates along the coast,
and in the speckled silence offers time
to breathe, unwitnessed,

waiting for the creature to emerge
at last from the shade
of seagrass, as itself, clear of the crude
rainbowy oil of his language.

Stone tongue | ANNE ELVEY

*after Jesper Svenbro 'A Critique of Pure Representation'
and 'Material for a Geological Theory of Language'*

Immersed in speech before you knew
tongue. Ear to your own cry's
primary exhalation. That tiny cave of bone.

Its tympani formed during your first
swim, tethered to tissue inside her pelvic
cage – osseous cells. Honeycomb. Rigid.

Porous. Surprisingly mobile. Expanding
to grasp you and let you go – slow as
your need, all being well. What

ancient stone-carved god imagined this
contraction and departure into world's
genealogy of flesh? The toes stubbed

on the mineral throb of becoming. You
with your toothless voice a younger
sibling of mountains and their caverns

cool with percolated lime. Windshaped
miracles of gravity. Their eons
echo in the barest bones of things

The day I opened the letter, the sky was cloudless, the blue unbroken. That night I found my crumpled car in the back corner of a restaurant. The customers took it away piece by piece. I forgot to take photos for the insurance. Next thing I was in in surgery. They removed the wrong baby. Another night my mother was young again. It was her wedding day. I couldn't find a dress to wear. I stood at the open wardrobe pushing bent necks along the rail, one way and then the other. The empty clothes were a grandfather's dead weight: tobacco-brown tweed, corduroy. Finally I found a dress. My arms disobeyed, my body wouldn't go through the right holes. As soon as I got it on, my sisters appeared in identical dresses. The day I opened the letter, the blue called out, *remember, nothing is yours, even if he fights you for it:* not the comforting hills, not the tree-ferns that brighten the gullies, not the slaters minding their business under the woodpile. The blue insisted, *look through me, look again,* even at the tiger snake at your heel, coiled in its magnificent defence.

The Blues | PETER GOLDSWORTHY

1.

I feel sorry for your father,
Granny told me after the funeral
of my newborn brother.
He can never show his feelings.
I had no idea
what she was talking about
since I wasn't invited.

2.

Your mother is staying in hospital
a few weeks longer, he explained
as he cooked breakfast
for the first time ever.
She's feeling a bit tired.

3.

Why did he die, Dad?
my other little brother
asked him as he cooked tea
for the first time ever.
Because he was a blue baby.
What's a blue baby, Dad?
That's enough questions
for now.

4.

The pretty Italian girl I shared
a desk with in Grade 5
had Burnt Umber eyes, Olive
skin and 72 Derwent pencils
in a wide flat tin including
12 thrilling shades of blue.
Why are you crying?
she asked as I coloured in
a Little Boy Blue. *Who's
crying?* I snapped back,
choosing Turquoise first,
then Cobalt Blue, adding
after careful thought,
a finishing touch
of Ultramarine.

5.

*Would you like
an early minute today,*
Peter, my teacher Mrs
Pikert asked. *Yes please,
Mum,* I said. I sometimes
called her Mum
my mistake.

The Creature Called Longing | JENNIFER KORNBERGER

Somewhere in a street crowded
with reason, my longing breaks free
from the leash and lumbers off to find you.

Shopkeepers guard their doorways
guessing the size of the creature's feet.

I climb to the top of the carpark
to spot it loitering in the botanical gardens.

Approaching from the Proteaceae, I linger
in full view, hoping it will be drawn
to my familiar scent,

but it sees me grip the harness
and shakes itself before lunging
for the underground.

I live for a time without longing:
the moon is distant, crater-less,

several maps are drawn from every conversation
but no arrow indicates *you are here.*

All wandering and calling, all searching of Rumi
for Shams finally gives over to blood tests, the need

to find something measurable in the body
that corresponds to these events.

Meanwhile, my longing negotiates systems
of transport, whimpering or howling at gangways;

no one seems prepared to call the police
because of its eloquent gestures,
the beginnings of speech in its eyes.

It's wearing a coat made from the fur
of every animal; when wild is sewn
to wild, a delicate balance ensues,

the only danger— its capacity
for feelings of orchestral intensity.

Untutored, it is making its way towards you;
I fear it will stand at your gates, rock back
and forth, like a Yeti, issuing gymnastic vowels.

Not knowing its origins, it will invest
you with exclusive meaning, adopt
a fragmentary grammar;

it will arrive without a name
or lineage, naked of prospects.

Don't open your iron gate, not yet.
Let my longing camp outside
under the zodiac— ram, bull, lion,
each one grunting its script in the dark;

through the bars, point out the river
of darkness that flows between
the known pictograms. Every night,

until I arrive at your mansion, redraw
the map of desire, dot-to-glimmering-dot,

stutter the names of these new constellations—
teach my longing the stories
that love has yet to tell.

Give it a reason for being,
even now, when it is just

a punctuation of stars
in the pelt of the logos.

The dark horse power, II | THOM SULLIVAN

To say nothing of [/something of] the songs
that haunt the stereo: haint blue, or

a shade of sainted cerulean, so dejected
that their notes upon the stave chart out
minor constellations. To say nothing of
[/or something for] the late-night talkback
callers who carry on a colloquy
between the songs: *This is Rich calling*
from Richmond, &/or This is Big Al calling

from Banka Banka on the Stuart Highway.
What these melodies won't cure you of
isn't worth curing, or wasn't worth having,
or not at this hour – what [/commuter]
thoughts, or what regressions. The night
is somewhere standing at the kerb,
trading words, trading gestures – or, elsewhere,

it's a silver station-wagon at a roadside,
hazards on, with its boot left open. And no one –
no, no one, & still no one. Still. A hyper-
focal, long exposure, in which every passing car
leaves a signature, a tracer, a single shot
into the dark, amid a squall of image noise
& bokeh. Freudenfreude for Jimmy

in Austin, TX, & godspeed to my sister
who's departing Birmingham, AL, at any hour.
Via Las Vegas. Via LA. Via Sydney.
The world converges, is [re]converging, just
as we [re]conceive of it. Even, always, now.

Immanence redirected. The infrastructure of the edgelord and the snowflake are the same.

Can power be generally oppressive? Up in the trees, radically outside the gift economy, radically outside bricolage. Read this sentence. Read this sentence linguistically. Tampering mid-ride.

Gusto prevailed once. Mulching depended upon it. Love, lovers, loving: such topics to while away the long winter evenings, when beaux came tripping on the windowsill. Light-hearted pet names give the measure of the domestic. I had two budgies, one called Left-wing, the other one Right-wing, they flew about the pots, smacked me when I was naughty. They died around the same time, and I drove out of town to bury them. Life felt game-less with them gone.

Buggies began to trend, like vinyl, uncontroversial 'clean roads and waterways', but dig a little deeper. The disappearance of cash created a push against the (heavily gendered) hip pocket economy. It was only after the war that my grandfather opened up to German philosophy, to the point of religiosity. Or theosophy. In the dark, he would ask, Johann Gottfried von Herder, should I travel this weekend, or, do I have bronchitis? Karma, to allude further, of sorts.

In the same way, or rather, with a similar attitude, I talk to birds, but I do it in the light, and I don't make a ceremony of it, I might be washing up. Violins play from neighbour's apartments. French horns, very occasionally. Swing low; in fact, land, if you want me to get on. Skiing is the most magical (holy) sport around.

Passing underfoot, the current wrecked me. I'm
alive
  with the cinema of it all. The wretched followers
in my wake. All I did was
coin this derivative slogan, among riverine
dramas,
  but the problem of slogans, they march to a
steady footfall. The problem of a steady footfall: I
resent the planked bridge
we're piling up—it's a station of
  certain loss.

                come with me if

Each evening, the number four would ring in my
head: begin every sentence: Four-get it! Come
round later.

                                For it is so...
  For the rest of us …
Four wild cherry ballart angling, earnest (you
remain wary)

I'll meet Lucy at the pool soon. I've given up a
foot, I might kick my way down a
lane or two
A teal plastic pump chipped off
        probably very far away now. Don't imagine
it—

We're trekking.
I've gathered chords.
Laces revive us.
              ahead the ghost peaks

Goretex, slapped on, resplendent, scoping heavy elevation while it rains girls. Prefer a prance over stalk, but botany reigns and the rooted are done with metaphor.

Cradling mere geodes, flanking to suffer our hot chicken summer. Collar the necks. Reading was never so useless!

A henchman loaded up her sack; we sang in 6/8 & derivative slogans dissolve

A henchman berated the stragglers, they did not hear her. What sort of pilgrimage
      fires its bodyguards? Are we not wretched enough?

The Language of Flowers | ALI JANE SMITH

The very glossy dark leaves of camellias
mean 'boredom'

the papery bougainvillea
means 'turning out better than expected'

and the yellow and white frangipani flowers
mean 'get it while you can'.

Some things
are strange, but not interesting.

Some biscuits
are only 'Nice', not 'Niece'.

Tonight the surf club is a dojang and people have gathered together
in their glamorous martial arts suits, sparring courteously.

Our laundry and the Parthenon
are both still standing, no thanks to the golden mean.

The dream you had that your bins moved in the night?
It's coming true. Hear the rolling wheels on the guilty footpath?

There was something before or after. Or. And.
Possum sits in the driveway.

Possum runs up a tree, but I can still see possum.
Possum doesn't act too worried.

The bird is like the tree, the bird is like the flower
the wallaby's fur is the colour of shadowed bark.

Been a predator? Prey? Know that likeness
means you'll go hungry

unlikeness means
you'll feel the snap of jaws.

Be a metaphor
or feel your own flesh rip.

Where's Pop? He's down the back. Oh.
Digging onion weed out of the lawn with a butter knife.

Onion weed means something's really given Pop the shits.
In the morning, back to normal.

I'm writing happy middlings.
Endings can be downers, easy ways out, or revelations

but I'd like endings
to be estuaries, full of nests.

The Scar | ISABELLA G. MEAD

In the aftermath, my friend asks me
how I will explain the scar to C.

Could you say it was a shark bite?
She's not serious but I consider it anyway—

the shark, arrow tipped in brown iodine,
blood-trained. Narrow eyes focus

like a needle trailing red silk. Later, my hands
attend the honeycomb dressing. Each gauzed

hexagon gleams—the wound below a gummy smile
thinning into permanence. Of course, the story

won't hold water—the scar a ruled line and not
a cartoon flower chomp. Its precision studied,

the opposite of any creature born from a salt purse.
C wouldn't believe me anyway.

See how she observes my lips as I speak?
The direction of my gaze will give me away—

not out to sea but directly ahead, eye to blue
eye. She'll recognise it at once. Her personal

entry point—tissue-white, tensile as a diving board.

The Stone | *JUDITH BEVERIDGE*

i.m. Dorothy Porter

A motorboat's propellor chops like a machete across the tide
sending a swift, breaking wave to the shore. I walk slowly
over rocks that are scored, overhung by a low, acned cliff.
In one of the rockpools an octopus stretches away
like a kitchen glove pulled from a hand. Soon dusk will arrive
with its shadows and mood lighting, but I'll stay and walk
to the jetty's end where a few fishermen compete for fish—
hauling them in or tossing the small ones back like tarnished cutlery.
On our last visit here—we hid a special stone under the pier,
gave it potency with our thanks and blessings, our hopes
for the future. I can still see you on the sand looking
for the right stone, grey and anonymous until you gathered it up
in the evening light and found the words to turn it into a talisman.
Now a darter takes flight, and I wonder what we might have
done that day had we known time would be a bird drowning
its wings. We might have put a feather under the wharf
and watched the tide carry it onto the blister-lines of foam.
I wonder if it's still there, our wish-bearing stone, or has
the water's drag taken it elsewhere. It wouldn't be right to look.
Still, I mourn you dear friend. You would have loved the eagle
flying overhead: its circles of flight—ripples from a well-laid stone.

Trans Pastoral | JOEL KEITH

How to tell
cut rock
from the natural wall
of the gorge?

Or the ducks
from the moorhens
plopped atop the screen-sheen
of gorge water?

Their wakes enclose
the lake in wide
parentheses.
The swimmers swim

and chatter with a
naturalness
whose opposite is
what you are

and which therefore
is all that you
desire. Their towels
flutter

like flags held to
change, flutter and
fly. What,
what is it to be

born
in that bright nation? And *not*
to be—only to guess at it

and, guessing, have
to reach toward—what
tragic blessing?

they slit the breast and insert a metal coil
so the future can always find the past

in the play the character dreams
of lying under an oak tree

there was a suspicious mass that turned out
not so suspicious but they wanted to mark the spot

at the hospital they tell her not to exercise
for three days and no baths or swimming

nothing that might make the bleeding start again
in the foyer at interval the audience murmurs

about their dull lives and how the resort in Nusa Dua
has its own private beach

the site aches in a low-level way like a reminder
of all the poor beleaguered breast has been through

in the play they all speak quickly and definitively
like people from the olden days

the reviewer calls it a once in a decade five-star work
why does it make her so angry that people like the play

is it because it is not a good play it is an okay play
and the superlatives distract from actual engagement with the play

she leaves the dressing on for a week and then peels it away
the bruising is yellow like autumn leaf stain

she puts the dressing in the bin and sees how she is not a person
but an amalgam of all the people she has known

the main thrust of the play is about a non-conforming woman
who has a consuming love for one man

there is not a more conforming story in all of the stories
she recalls how the radiographers during her earlier treatments

were mostly young men
looking at her breasts day after day laid out flat

with tiny tattoos on her chest guiding the young men
as to where to fire the radiation

she fought hard against feeling passive and objectified
she took photos of the breast the tattoos the bruises all of it

she recalls the day she saw the black plastic covered body
on the drive to the hospital

it was the same day she learned that Olivia Newton-John
had died

the day she learned she had cancer she remembered
how she had adored Olivia as a kid how she had sung along

to *Hopelessly Devoted to You* and *Physical* in her Dad's study
wearing the big headphones

some days strange things hurt like the vein in her wrist
where they always try to draw blood

today there were two women in day oncology with a tiny baby
and a sandwich

does the baby have cancer she wondered
or one of the women and is one of them the baby's mother

she doesn't remember how the plays ends
even while applauding the effort she starts to forget

outside the theatre after the show it is raining
that February rain a relief on their hot February skin

Twilight | LUOYANG CHEN

Kini ia meminta kembali Musim Hujan
Dan aku kembalikan semua
Dan aku kembali Semu

—NORMAN ERIKSON PASARIBU

I

A summer's (s)trip across the Indian Ocean—

I want to understand currency like I understand tranquillity.

The way your Adam's apple moves as you are talking—I feel my eyes
most present, and watery. Your hands on my back, rubbing aloe vera
on my sunburnt body. My shoulders tighten. My hands stiffen. Fearful
of my old habits/violation. My heart stopped for a few minutes.
Wanting protection of you from me. I am not horny.

A broken letter with a breaking heart. You tell me that the average
wage in Bali is between $200 and $300 AUD per month. How dare I
even say *If one day you come to Australia...* to you. O my twilight—

You tell me *Keep your mind straight, and you'll be alright*. I manoeuvre
around the table, then the ocean. The rain gives you fever on your ride
to work. I see your face in every puddle. I want to say—

Park your motorbike
Here, under the tree.
Parkir motor,
Twilight.
But I act cool, and say *No big deal.*

II

Hello from the other side—

Of course it is a big deal. Of course it is about geography. Of course
it is queer. There's an ocean you can never truly cross, no matter how
much your body sweats, you say. You say, *It's hard, but I am happy.*
The 9–5 non-stop wiping of wet floor. The constant sound of a blowing
whistle. The organised chaos. Tokay gecko chirping. I am in Bali but
won't be for long.

III

Stench of confinement
A certain attachment:
Untidy scene—servile
Damaged
In this blessed world

I don't want to… I…
Can I… May I… Shall I… Must I…
I wish I…

Ample debris
Falls
Weakly
Lack of aspiration—

                                            Rot

Imagine the last scene:
Anachronistic—

The way he listened, across the ocean, so closely
Maudlin and feverish

At some point

The waves splash
The look's coming apart at the seams

Ocean, ocean…
In my stomach

This is how the ocean dazzles speech
This is how a blink lets go of the urge

IV

On my day
of departure
for Australia,
you ask me
for a photo
of us.
You ask me
to return.
I won't return
in full.
I will return in full.

V

The ocean is

- not a motif.
- an ocean.
- actual.
- vast.
- not sorry.
- not sorry.

Note: The epigraph is from Norman Erikson Pasaribu's short story collection *Cerita-cerita Bahagia, Hampir Seluruhnya* (Gramedia Pustaka Utama, 2020), which is used in this poem with the author's permission. 'Hello from the other side' is direct quote from English singer-songwriter Adele's song-lyric 'Hello', which was released on 23 October 2015 by XL Recordings as the lead single from her third studio album, 25 (2015).

Two Poems Shot on iPhone | LUKE PATTERSON

i. Lizard

You were dormant and now the water
dragon, unflinching on a white rock—

It's Dharug today, but tomorrow's Gumbanggir
will give another lizard.

The lizard was just that and I search
uncle Google for all his names including the latinate

because poetry likes it. I want to call his belly terra-
cotta but I call it deep red ochre instead.

There it is: *Intellagama lesueurii*, meaning 'intelligent
lizard'. How about that!?

ii. Turkey

Oh, mighty Turkey
of the Brush! I'm sure I know
your face. Creation Being, twice now
our paths cross.

I fell in deprecation,
spoke in tongue and gobbledygook,
for you. I shooed the cat gods
and gave the bird

to my neighbour. I declared
ketchup and mustard
as my totems when once-
upon-a-time I'd say nothing!

Oh, mighty Turkey
moving mountains with
your strut. Here now, again
I'm your egg buried in a mound.

Untitled | PETER O'MARA

✝

b.

uneven

hills │

Proserpina

abrupt, the

collusion

of Gods, uneasy

icons, death

& rebirth.

joy

and sorrow.

thou

breast of love

.

│ grow.

Upon the Passing of Tomas Tranströmer | JOEL EPHRAIMS

The world has come up to my window
to tell me it's not too late
to tell me yes yes you too are still alive.

The gods and demons of the Śatapathabrāhmaṇa
have left their terrestrial lids
along with their creation, destruction saliva
in recesses of the purple altocumulus wood
where my monkey-self swings
watching serotine bubbles column
like oil from disappeared planes.

How often I have felt like a gaudy insect
in those gloomy, effulgent kitchens
where gods and demons and poems
loom above my rare lamb steak
and the profundity is knowing
that they too will overlook the resplendent fur
that trellises me but I can't separate.

My head anti-missile chaffs and flares
and it feels like the tails of the comets are conspiring
against me in my latest dark irrationality.
Or is it my super awareness? It is it is in this fringe of the park
which is a page the drug lords also read.

I will refuse to be wolves beyond my white banishment.
I will walk up the banistered puddles
of echoed houses as the senses of an incorporeal cube,
not slowing down.

The sleeper trains are mating.
The slender comets have treacled from their sky warrens
to be folded arm-over-arm
and fused with closed hands as sun is into the grass.

Today it feels like sundown.
The islands look violent and majestic.
All the gravitational fire
and all the gravitational black.

1.

He was generous to a fault, i.e. talentless,
in bin-skittled dawn despair tolerantly tracks
a siren's perfect 4th
through birds' helix'd calls.

Downstairs he dreams wheels savoured on a pension.
Flats tilt,
tenants hustle the walkways.
Unreadable, the breach notice gags,
head in bucket.

2.

On the book the photo of a saint's see-no-evil eyes culls reception.
A picnic rug
hails the letters wiped of poison,
the street's antiseptic flowers and dismembered trees.
The bank statement says *I am a bank.*

The leader reads autocues like lunch
in his ziggurat,
the vanquished dead sail on the walls.
A caravanserai slugs its invented interlocutor.

3.

Keep to short and acrid.
Dread the infinite.
The lugubrious voice quaked to selfhood
obliterates the painting.

4.

Two drinks and she's anyone's
Anyone's anecdote she fills with herself.
Night shrieked, dawn bled,
mauve and yellow sky calibrates time.
Watch the film for the music, the series for the city,
among the impotent wars' crunched rebuke,
the friendship braceleteers, ethnographers and amnesiacs,
expect little and get it.

Watching the Lightning Strike | SHEY MARQUE

Come is the day light leaves a birdless place,
nuclei of heavy atoms blasted
into the cloud by an exploding star,
and let's say the light pulse could look outward
from the nucleus—it would see a field
of faster time, and you might see a freak
mirror of yourself. You can't look away.
Silent rays are sparking from sky to skin—
star-light synapses faster than a thought
shower down on the welkin of the earth,
pass right through us while our eyes are smitten,
and doesn't this change you, doesn't this change
the way you evolve, how it edits you,
the way you're read, one letter at a time.

We are become | MICAELA SAHHAR

From her hospital bed my aunt remembers
communion at our local parish; *the Muslims
cared for it*, she says, in the Christian Quarter
gone days of their orthodoxy at

the Church of the Holy Sepulchre. *Mum said,
'don't spit!'* she laughs, the taste of communion
wine catching in the memory of her throat, there
in incense   and here,   the word.

*

In the times of the Abbasid, al-Hallaj declares
Ana al Haqq[i]   this was when words mattered;
he may have been decapitated or otherwise
hanged; where the cremains were scattered,

pilgrims came, until this too was washed away
(a torrential ecstasy, the Sufi's divination). Much later
a journalist will say that imprisonment, exile or
decapitation   *is how you can tell the words matter.*

*

At an award ceremony: resistance
is quietly attired saying,   this book *is both
a book about protests, and one that acts
as a protest.*[ii] Swathed in no visible symbols

but language is about him, articles become an
armoury of liberation; June Jordan[iii] stands behind,
I am become a Palestinian (after Sabra after
Shatila)   balanced on a y shaped frame.

*

Repaired by a team internationally assembled,
in 2015; the BBC described[iv] it as *neglected*.
But the French technician muttered *everything
is dead!* examining (230 strings, 88 hammers) the body

of the instrument, the canopy of Nawras Theatre exploded
by Israel's bombs, (a La Scala of apocalypse) beneath
a gaping sky where sunset does not come; the pianoforte
inventory presumed an upright, instead,   a miracle.

*

Hurra (on my tshirt)   as in, *Hurra Hurra Falastin!* As in
From the Yarra to Port Philip Bay! As in   *From
Birrarung to Nerm* (later flooded by sea)   as in
bahr   (as in hurra from censorship)   as in

we remember. One day there will be nothing left
to describe the feeling of what they did. Only that
we loved each child we never met and read their
names   until   an intifada became a thawra;

and everywhere, becoming.

Endnotes:
i.   Muddasir Ramzan (2023). "'Making up stories is an inherently political act': Mohsin Hamid in conversation.' *Journal of Postcolonial Writing*, 59 (1), pp. 113–24; 118.
ii. Giramondo Publishing (2025). 'Hasib Hourani's *rock flight* wins the Kenneth Slessor Prize for Poetry.' May 19: https://giramondopublishing.com/hasib-hourani-rock-flight-wins-kenneth-slessor-prize-for-poetry.
iii. June Jordan (2023). 'Moving Towards Home.' In *Living Room: New Poems.* Thunder's Mouth Press, p. 134.
iv. Tim Whewell (2015). 'Saving Gaza's Only Grand Piano.' *BBC News*, March 26: https://www.bbc.com/news/magazine-32042375#:~:text=The%20only%20concert%20grand%20piano,way%20for%20a%20rare%20concert.

We are young and delicious | STEPHANIE POWELL

young, delicious just like (we hope)

the girls in Dolly with the
thoroughbred manes and pin-drop legs, young and
delicious or so

boys outside the train station say.
We pass them in school

uniforms showering glances
like fists of confetti, filling eyes and mouths

spend our money on hot chips to share. Sometimes
we take the train into the city

to sit in Fed square
and undo our top buttons.

Tell the men who come
We are young and delicious, young and

delicious, when our youth doubles as a blessing and
an injury.
We will tell them to

empty themselves out
of praises until it is dinner time

and we must leave behind our *young and delicious*
go back to the suburbs.

Leave the threads of our song to simmer,
to wait, to ripen, to waste.

We could have gone wandering out into the snow
| ANDREW SUTHERLAND

We could have gone wandering out into the snow.
Something about the endless tundra of desire. A joke.
The joke of the poem. In diaspora Russian:
when you are alone, the sickness grabs you;
pulls you down. With others, you are let free.
But do we feel it any less?   We could have

offered a man a tip then gone wandering out
onto the cobbled stone. We could have stayed
drunk. Stayed sober. We could have fumbled
our best friend's wedding. Made a 1990s of
the scene. I'd like to tell you about the time
I was cast in a two-scene role in some sci-fi B movie

starring Kristen Stewart. She was my '*straight exception*'
(yes her and Rooney Mara) when I still thought that real
meant fixed in place and reel meant fixed in
time. Anyway. They wrote my character out
a few weeks before shooting. I don't know.
No proximity to Kristen, is what matters. I think it was

about people without feelings, getting feelings.
A bomb. There's no point to this history other
than to let people know. We could have filmed
ourselves in that slight desaturation sheen.
We could have been a camera angle. A shot.
We could have wandered out from tropics to the snow.

What Size is My Baby Poem | TOBY FITCH

Your baby is the size of a pollen grain.

Your baby is the size of a microbead in your ovary.

Your baby is the size of a chunk of rock salt.

Your baby is the size of the lithium-ion battery in your phone.

Your baby is the size of a bumblebee.

Your baby is the size of a Coca-Cola bottle cap, 110 billion
of which were manufactured last year.

Your baby is the size of a southern corroboree frog sucked up
into the Cloud and torrented back down.

Your baby is the size of a vape.

Your baby is the size of a monarch butterfly shuddering into
your diaphragm.

Your baby is the size of an undimmable restaurant filament bulb.

Your baby is the size of a pygmy possum.

Your baby is the size of a scrunched-up plastic bag.

Your baby is the size of an orange, the fruit of light.

Your baby is the size of a hamburger in a styrofoam container.

Your baby is the size of a macaw.

Your baby is the size of a flat basketball bouncing on the court of your pelvis.

Your baby is the size of an echidna in breech position.

Your baby is the size of a blackbox.

Your baby is the size of a watermelon.

Your baby is the size of a pirate ship Lego set.

Your baby is the size of a pangolin curled up in its armour.

Your baby is the size of one MK-84 bomb.

Your baby is the size of a snow leopard ghosting through the Himalayas.

Your baby is the size of a wheelie bin.

Your baby is the size of a hammerhead shark thrashing about in an amniotic ocean.

Your baby is the size of the oxygen tank of the crashed-landed Skylab on Oondiri country.

Your baby is the size of one of the four horses.

Your baby is the size of a Cybertruck.

Your baby is the size of a white rhino.

Your baby is the size of a Reaper drone, posterior position.

Your baby is the size of a blue whale.

Your baby is the size of a 5-bedroom beach-side penthouse left vacated by AirBnB landlords.

Your baby is the size of a memory of Sumatran elephants.

Your baby is the size of a nuclear reactor and is now engaged.

Your baby is the size of the Great Barrier Reef.

Your baby is the size of a country razed.

Your baby is the size of a Category-5 cyclone.

Your baby is the size of all human-made space junk in orbit around the globe.

Your baby is the size of Mars and is 3390 km dilated.

Your baby is the size of genocide.

When the world ends, there will be singing | ALISHA BROWN

After Motto *by Bertolt Brecht*

We will take our chairs and our coats and walk to the end of the street.

We will take our chairs and our coats and place them side by side

at a comfortable distance. We will greet the neighbours we know

and give our names to those we don't. We will say: I am sorry

for this or that. I wish I'd done so. I wish I'd not. We will say:

you are forgiven. The children will have rocks in their pockets

and the mothers will have food. There is no hope, but they are mothers.

The men will bring their dogs, who run unleashed through rows of legs

and bowl the toddlers over and lick sausage fat from barbecue tongs,

and they will not be punished. We will kiss our lovers and throw our phones

in a petrol tank. We will set it alight. The children will make shadow puppets

and someone's grandfather will play *Clair de Lune* on a maple piano

dragged by six teenage boys onto the bitumen. For the first time,

we will watch his hands. We will look at our own hands.

A cake will be brought for someone's birthday and the water will come only once the last candle is blown. When the power cuts, we won't know

who starts the song, and we won't know the words, but we will clear our throats

and splash our arms and sing. The sun will roll its hot body over the horizon.

We will cough. Touch our children's hair. Most will die instantly.

The chairs will float, and the last bird will make a small sound when it falls.

Wolsey Road | PETRA WHITE

A yellow wren builds a nest in the bare pear tree.
The child tracks its progress from the breakfast table,
wings shaking mid-air –
and in the kitchen air above her flaxen head
the intricate problems of adults
leap and swirl, careful to avoid landing.
When our suffering is over,
it will start up like a blaze,
and be mistaken for a sunset.
The sky, at certain times,
will be red with the suffering of countless others,
who will greet with both hands
the Bear that will come from the North,
as my parents used to say,
awaiting the Resurrection with biscuits and tea.
Where is North, I cry to their ancestors.
They cannot answer, their lips are sealed even for tea,
their eyes are sealed too, and they cannot watch us.
In the morning I wait for a train,
on the way to the interview,
husband and daughter appear on the other side
of the tracks, waving good luck,
like angels, child
grinning in her purple school uniform –
and him too, stooped beside her, both waving madly,
watching over me as I watch over them.

Work | *YEENA KIRKBRIGHT*

Work gets caught under fingernails
nestles in the rolled-up cuffs of pants
falls to the bedroom floor, ends up in bed.

Work becomes after hours in the lower back
curls up in the corners of lungs
becomes persistent, shortness of breath
gets trapped under a front-end loader
while scavenging in a landfill for beer.

Work is great for diversity reporting
has dark skin, won't look you in the eyes
won't join the union — our best work
ers. We built this great nation on the
back of work so black you didn't have
to pay for it.

Work has four core values and a vision
and its most important value is "integrity".

Hard work and dedication are desirable
they are fit and young and "collaborating"
in work toilets, you want to be them.

Work seeps from pores, sits beading on brows
is always on time at the dinner table
sprinkling waking hours like salt, 29.4%.

It's important that work stays at home
during those first developing years
so a house and a car can be purchased
so work can fund the posing of holiday snaps.

Work turns 65, retires, divorces from an
unpaid lifetime of work, now with 24% less super.

Work is a good corporate citizen
always wipes up afterwards
always assists authorities
with investigations.

CONTRIBUTORS
& ACKNOWLEDGEMENTS

Notes on Contributors

Adam Aitken taught cultural studies and creative writing for many years in Sydney, and his most recent book is *Revenants* (Giramondo Publishing, 2022), which was shortlisted for the Kenneth Slessor Prize. He won the Patrick White Award in 2021.

Alice Allan produced the long-running podcast *Poetry Says.* Her work has appeared in *HEAT, Overland, Island,* and the *Sydney Review of Books.* Her debut collection *The Empty Show* was shortlisted for the Anne Elder Award.

Amanda Anastasi is a Melbourne poet and author of *Taking Apart the Bird Trap* (Recent Work Press, 2024) and *The Inheritors* (Black Pepper Publishing, 2021). Amanda was Poet in Residence for three years at the Monash Climate Change Communication Research Hub, and her poetry featured in COP30 Brazil's Global Ethical Stocktake for the Oceania region. She has been the recipient of a Wheeler Centre Hot Desk Fellowship and published in journals locally and internationally, including in *Australian Poetry Journal, Griffith Review, Cordite Poetry Review, The Massachusetts Review* and *Best Australian Science Writing.*

Chris Andrews lives on Gadigal-Wangal land. Third book of poems: *The Oblong Plot* (Puncher & Wattmann, 2024). *Study of the Oulipo: How to Do Things with Forms* (McGill-Queen's University Press, 2022). Recent translations: *I Don't Care* by Ágota Kristóf (New Directions, 2024) and *You Glow in the Dark* by Liliana Colanzi (New Directions, 2024).

Alison J Barton is a Wiradjuri poet working on Wurundjeri land. Her first full-length collection of poetry, *Not Telling,* was published by Puncher & Wattmann. You can read more about her at www.alisonjbarton.com

Stuart Barnes' most recent poetry collection, *Like to the Lark* (Upswell Publishing), was awarded the 2023 Wesley Michel Wright Prize, shortlisted for the 2024 ALS Gold Medal and highly commended in the 2024 Kenneth Slessor Prize. Stuart's a member of Hell Herons, a spokenword+music collective whose first album, *The Wreck Event,* is out now.

Judith Beveridge was born in London, England in 1956 and moved to Sydney, Australia in 1960 where she has lived ever since. Her first book, *The Domesticity of Giraffes,* was published in 1987 and won major prizes. Since then, she has published seven volumes. *Sun Music: New and Selected Poems* (Giramondo Publishing, 2018) won the Prime Minister's Award for Poetry in 2019. She taught poetry writing for 16 years at Sydney University and was the poetry editor of *Meanjin* for 10 years. Her work has been studied in universities and schools and has won numerous awards. *Tintinnabulum* is her latest book (Giramondo Publishing, 2024).

Kevin Brophy's latest book is the poetry collection, *An Inventory of Longing* (Whitmore Press, 2025). Kevin is patron of the Melbourne Poets Union, and in 2021 he was awarded an Order of Australia (AM) for his services to creative writing and education.

Alisha Brown is a writer, editor, and musician born on Kamilaroi land with ties to Wonnarua, Yuin, and Gadigal Country. She won the 2022 Joyce Parkes Women's Writing Prize, placed second in the 2021 Woorilla Poetry Prize, and was nominated for a Pushcart Prize. She has also appeared in many SCWC anthologies and was Highly Commended for the 2024 and 2025 SCWC Poetry Prizes. You can find her work in *Westerly*, *Griffith Review*, *Cordite*, the *Australian Poetry Anthology*, and *Meanjin*, among others. She was a featured artist in the 2024 Emerging Writers' Festival and works for *The Suburban Review* as Submissions Manager.

Lachlan Brown teaches English and Creative Writing at Charles Sturt University. His poems have appeared in *The Weekend Australian, Cordite, Australian Book Review*, and *Rabbit*. He has been shortlisted and commended for various prizes including the Gwen Harwood Poetry Prize, the Peter Porter Poetry Prize and the Blake Poetry Prize. In 2021 Lachlan won the Newcastle Poetry Prize. Lachlan has worked on exhibitions with visual and photographic artists including Dr Tony Curran (Limiting Entropy) and James Farley (Walking in Isolation). Lachlan's poetry includes works created in response to commissions from the Powerhouse Museum and ABC Everyday.

Pam Brown has been active in the Australian poetry scene in diverse modes for five decades. A number of her many books have been on the shortlists and have sometimes won the prize. Her most recent collection of poems, *Guess the Experience*, was published by Hunter Publishers in October 2025. Pam lives on Gadigal land.

Bonny Cassidy is author of three collections of poetry and one book of nonfiction, and has been shortlisted for the Prime Minister's Literary Awards, Victorian Premier's Literary Awards and the ALS Gold Medal. Bonny is an internationally recognised scholar and critic of Australian poetry and literature, and leads workshops and mentorship for writers. She is currently working on a second book of nonfiction, and has recently won the AAALS Creative Prose Prize 2025. She lives in the bush on Dja Dja Wurrung Country.

Derek Chan holds an MFA from Cornell University, where he was a university fellow, an editor of EPOCH, and a two-time recipient of the Corson-Browning Poetry Prize. His work has appeared or is forthcoming in *New England Review, Best of Australian Poems, Oxford Poetry, The Margins*, and elsewhere. He was a finalist for the 2024 Forward Prize for the Best Single Written Poem, and the 2025 Tin House residency. He has received fellowships from Vermont Studio Centre and has been shortlisted for awards by *Frontier Poetry, The Adroit Journal*, and *Palette Poetry*. He teaches creative writing and composition at Cornell University.

Luoyang Chen is a Chinese poet living and working in Australia. He is the author of *Flow* (Red River/Centre for Stories, 2023) and *And the Waves* which is forthcoming with Puncher and Wattmann. Luoyang's poems have also been published in literary journals such as *Cordite Poetry Review, Rabbit, Plumwood Mountain Journal, The Suburban Review*, and *Overland*.

Eileen Chong is an Australian poet who was born in Singapore of Hokkien, Hakka and Peranakan (Straits Chinese) descent. She is the author of 11 books. Her work has been shortlisted for numerous prizes, including the Victorian Premier's Literary Award, the NSW Premier's Literary Award and twice for the Prime Minister's Literary Award. She is the 2025 recipient of the Shanghai Writers' Program Western Sydney University Fellowship and the 2026 recipient of a BR Whiting Studio Residency in Rome, Italy. Her most recent books are *We Speak of Flowers* (UQP, 2025) and *Notes on Tomb-Sweeping* (Life Before Man, 2024). She lives and works on unceded land of the Gadigal people.

Ali Cobby Eckermann's first collection *little bit long time* launched her literary career in 2009. In 2014 Ali was the first Aboriginal Australian writer to attend the International Writing Program at University of Iowa. In 2016 Ali presented a Keynote at the Active Aesthetics conference in Berkeley California, and presented at Christchurch Writers Festival New Zealand. In 2017 Ali received a Windham-Campbell Award from Yale University, and presented at Vancouver Writers Festival. Her latest release *She Is The Earth* won the Indigenous Writers Prize and Book of The Year at the 2024 NSW Premier's Literary Awards.

Aidan Coleman teaches at Southern Cross University (Gold Coast campus) where he is the Coordinator for Creative Writing. His collections of poetry, *Avenues & Runways* (2005), *Asymmetry* (2012) and *Mount Sumptuous* (2020) have been shortlisted for national book awards. A biography, *Thin Ice: A life of John Forbes*, is in press with Melbourne UP.

Emilie Collyer lives on unceded Wurundjeri Country where she writes across forms. She has two poetry collections published by Vagabond Press: *Do you have anything less domestic?* (winner Five Islands Prize) and *As If I'm Really There*. Her poetry has been recognised in Gwen Harwood, Judith Wright and Newcastle poetry prizes. Her play *Super* premiered at Red Stitch in 2025 and she is currently under commission with The Street (Canberra).

Amy Crutchfield is a poet. Her work has been published in Australia, the UK and Ireland. Her first collection, *The Cyprian* (Giramondo), was published in 2023 and received the Prime Minister's Literary Award in 2024.

Madeleine Dale is a poet and PhD candidate. She holds first-class honours and a Masters degree in Creative Writing from the University of Queensland. Her first full-length collection, *Portraits of Drowning*, won the 2023 Thomas Shapcott Prize and was commended in the Wesley Michel Wright Prize. She was a 2024 MacDowell Fellow.

Natalie Damjanovich-Napoleon is a writer, songwriter, and educator raised on a farm by Croatian-immigrant parents. Her poetry and nonfiction have appeared in *Meanjin, Cordite, ABR*, and *APJ*. She's won the Bruce Dawe and KSP Poetry Prizes, and was shortlisted for the Peter Porter Prize. Her second poetry book, *If There Is a Butterfly That Drinks Tears*, was released by Life Before Man/Gazebo Books. A #1 ARIA-charting songwriter, her work has featured on NPR and alongside US Poet Laureate Ada Limón. Natalie teaches creative writing and ESL, and volunteers with the WA Poets committee.

Jelena Dinic arrived in Australia in 1993 during the collapse of Yugoslavia. She writes in Serbian and English. Her first poetry collection *In the room with the she wolf* was selected for the Adelaide Festival 2020 Premier's Unpublished Manuscript Award and was the winner of the Mary Gilmore Award in 2022. She lives in the Adelaide Hills with her family.

Michelle D'Souza is the author of three collections of poetry and fiction and has received prizes such as the Val Vallis Award, the Red Room Poetry Fellowship and the NSW Premier's Literary Award for New Writing for *Letter to Pessoa*. Her poems have appeared in *Southerly, Meanjin, The Kenyon Review* and *The London Magazine*.

Laurie Duggan was involved in the poetry worlds of Melbourne and Sydney through the 1970s and 80s, publishing several books of poems and a critical work *Ghost Nation: Imagined Space and Australian Visual Culture* (2001). He taught media studies, art history, and cultural studies at various institutions. In 2006 he moved to the UK and lived in Faversham, Kent until 2018 after which he returned to Sydney. His most recent books are *Homer Street* (Giramondo, 2020) and *Selected Poems 1971–2017* (Shearsman, 2018).

Anne Elvey lives on unceded Bunurong Country, as a settler descendent of Irish, Scottish and English ancestry. Her most recent poetry collections are *(C) loud: A poetic response to child sexual abuse in the Roman Catholic church* (Palaver, 2025), *Intents* (Liquid Amber Press, 2025), *Leaf* (Liquid Amber Press, 2022) and *Obligations of Voice* (Recent Work Press, 2021). Her work spans ecological poetry and poetics, ecological feminist hermeneutics, environmental and social justice, and unsettling settlerdom. Anne was inaugural managing editor of *Plumwood Mountain* journal until 2020. https://sunglintdrift.com/

Joel Ephraims's recent poetry books include *Biota*, published by Apothecary Archive in 2022 and *Flying Car Kaleidoscope*, published by Vagabond Press in 2024. His poetry has appeared in *Overland, The Weekend Australian, Cordite Poetry Review, Quadrant*, and *Griffith Review* among other places. He is currently working on a participatory and conceptual novel titled 15^{238} as part of his PhD thesis at the University of Sydney. 15^{238} will explore Natural Language Processing (NLP) artificial intelligence (AI) technology and its extensions and warpings of the tenuous social fabric of our times through play with the superhero genre, café counters, airs, sports, social media, idioms and footpaths among other radiant and overcast, ancient and immediate phenomena

Michael Farrell is from Bombala NSW and has lived in Melbourne since 1990. Recent book publications include *The Victoria Principle* (stories) and *Googlecholia* (poems). Michael edits *The Chalamet Review* and is poetry editor for *Westerly*.

Susan Fealy is a poet and clinical psychologist based in Naarm/Melbourne. Her debut collection *Flute of Milk* won the 2017 Wesley Michel Wright Prize and shortlisted for the ASAL 2018 Mary Gilmore Award. *The Deer Woman* is forthcoming with Upswell in 2026.

Toby Fitch (he/they) is a lecturer in creative writing at the University of Sydney, and former poetry editor of *Overland*. Author of eight books of poetry, including *Where Only the Sky had Hung Before* (2019), *Sydney Spleen* (2021) and *Object Permanence: Calligrammes* (2022), he is currently writing a book called *Endlings*. He lives on unceded Gadigal land with his partner, their three children and a staffy.

Holly Friedlander Liddicoat has previously been published in *Cordite, Overland, Rabbit, Southerly, The Lifted Brow* and *Voiceworks*, among others. She's edited poetry for *Voiceworks* and the *UTS Writers' Anthology*. Rabbit Poetry published her first collection *CRAVE*, which was shortlisted for the 2019 Mary Gilmore Award. In 2023 her manuscript *DOGHOUSE* was shortlisted for the Helen Anne Bell Bequest, and was published in 2025 with Vagabond Press.

Claire Gaskin lives on Bunurong country. Sovereignty has never been ceded. Her first full length poetry collection, *a bud*, was published by John Leonard Press in 2006. It was completed in the receipt of an Australia Council grant and shortlisted in the SA Festival Awards. Her subsequent collections are *Paperweight* (Hunter Publishers, 2013), *Eurydice Speaks* (Hunter Publishers, 2021), *Ismene's Survivable Resistance* (Puncher &Wattmann, 2021) and *Weather Event* (Gazebo Books, 2023). *Night Heart's Material Witness: Prose Poems* was completed in 2025 assisted by a Creative Australia grant and is forthcoming with Puncher & Wattmann. Gaskin is a long-term lecturer and facilitator of poetry courses across the tertiary and community sectors. She is available for private editing and mentoring at clairegaskinpoetry.com

Kerry Greer is a poet and writer based in Western Australia. She received the Venie Holmgren Prize for Environmental Poetry in 2021. She was awarded second place in the 2024 Elizabeth Jolley Short Story Prize run by *Australian Book Review*. Kerry has been shortlisted for the Calibre Essay Prize, the Woollahra Digital Literary Award, the Newcastle Poetry Prize, the ACU Poetry Prize, the Gwen Harwood Poetry Prize, and more. She holds an MFA in Poetry from Cedar Crest College. Her debut poetry collection, *The Sea Chest*, was published by Recent Work Press in 2023.

Peter Goldsworthy's numerous literary awards include the Commonwealth Poetry Prize, and the Australian Bicentennial Prize for Poetry (shared with Phillip Hodgins). His poems have been widely published in the English-speaking world, from journals such as *Poetry* magazine and *The London Review of Books* to anthologies ranging from *The Twentieth Century in Poetry* to Roger McGough's recently edited *Happy Poems*. His poems can be read and heard online at The Poetry Archive.

Elena Gomez is the author of *Admit the Joyous Passion of Revolt* and *Body of Work*. She lives on unceded Wurundjeri country.

Natalie Harkin (Narungga) is a poet and creative arts-based Research Fellow with the Indigenous Studies team at Flinders University, Kaurna Yarta. She is passionate about archival justice, engaging archival-poetic methods to document community Memory Stories, domestic labour history, and Indigenous Living-Legacy archive innovations for our time. Her books include *Dirty Words* (Cordite Books, 2015), *Archival-poetics* (Vagabond Press, 2019), and *APRON-SORROW / SOVEREIGN-TEA* (Wakefield Press, 2025).

Jennifer Harrison has written eight books of poetry, most recently *Anywhy* (Black Pepper, 2018). Four new collections *Sideshow History, Finials, Fowler's Phrenology* and *wOmens wOrk* will appear from Australian publishers in 2025/2026/2027. Her most recent prize is the 2024 Heroines International Poetry Prize (co-winner). She chairs the World Psychiatry Association's Section for Art and Psychiatry.

Dominique Hecq is a widely anthologised and award-winning poet, fiction writer, essayist and translator. Her creative works comprise a novel, six collections of short stories and seventeen books of poetry. Together with *Volte Face* and *Otopos* her bilingual sequence, *Pistes de rêve* appeared in 2024. *Errances* is slated for 2026. Among other recent honours Dominique Hecq is a recipient of the International Best Poets Prize administered by the International Poetry Translation and Research Centre in conjunction with the International Academy of Arts and Letters and the James Tate Prize for poetry.

Hasib Hourani is a Lebanese-Palestinian writer, editor, arts worker and educator living on Gadigal Country in Sydney. His work has been published in *Meanjin, Overland, Australian Poetry* and *Cordite*, among others. He is a 2020 recipient of The Wheeler Centre's Next Chapter Scheme and his 2021 essay, 'when we blink' was shortlisted for The *LIMINAL* & Pantera Press Nonfiction prize and published in their 2022 anthology, *Against Disappearance*. His debut book *rock flight* won the Kenneth Slessor Prize for Poetry and the Mary Gilmore Award in 2025, and was shortlisted for the Prime Minister's Literary Award for Poetry.

D.J. Huppatz lives and writes in Naarm/Melbourne, Australia. Recent work in *Ballast, Exacting Clam, Fugitives and Futurists, Variant Literature,* and *Gone Lawn*. He is the author of two poetry books, *Happy Avatar* (Puncher and Wattmann, 2015) and *Astroturfing for Spring* (Puncher and Wattmann, 2021). He also writes about design and architecture.

David Ishaya Osu is a poet, memoirist and street photographer living in South Australia. His work has appeared in *Rabbit, Island, Griffith Review, The Hopkins Review, The Oxford Review of Books,* among others. He is winner of the Charles Rischbieth Jury Poetry Prize for 2024 and is currently completing a PhD in Creative Writing at the University of Adelaide.

Holly Isemonger is a poet from Gerringong, NSW. She was the joint winner of the Judith Wright Poetry Prize. Her work has appeared in journals such as *Cordite, Blackbox Manifold, Overland* and *Westerly*. She is the author of *Greatest Hit* (Vagabond Press) and the chapbooks *Hip Shifts* (If A Leaf Falls Press) and *Deluxe Paperweight* (Stale Objects dePress).

Andy Jackson is a disabled poet, and lecturer in creative writing at the University of Melbourne. His latest poetry collection *Human Looking* won the ALS Gold Medal and the Prime Minister's Literary Award for Poetry. Andy is a co-editor of *Raging Grace: Australian Writers Speak Out on Disability* (Puncher & Wattmann, 2024), an anthology of collaborative poems and essays. He writes and rests on Dja Dja Wurrung country.

Gurmeet Kaur is a writer of poetry and criticism. Her work appears in *Debris, Rabbit, Island, Cordite, Liminal, Kill Your Darlings, Poetry Birmingham Literary Journal*, and elsewhere. She was Highly Commended in the 2024 Next Chapter Fellowship and awarded 2023 New Critic at *Kill Your Darlings*.

Joel Keith is a writer and musician living on unceded Wurundjeri land. Their work has appeared in *Overland, Island, Cordite* and *The Suburban Review*. She placed third in the Judith Wright Poetry Prize 2024. She is the editor of *Voiceworks*.

Anna Kerdijk Nicholson's most recent books are *True Wit & Beauty: Joe Byrne, Dan & Ned Kelly & Steve Hart* and *Dictat: poems in a time of autocracy* (both from Poesis Press, 2025). Her poetry has won major Australian prizes, both for *Possession* (her second book) and for individual poems. She farms in rural NSW.

The three volumes of **John Kinsella**'s collected poems are *The Ascension of Sheep* (UWAP, 2022), *Harsh Hakea* (UWAP, 2023) and *Spirals* (UWAP, 2024). His new collection of poetry is *Ghost of Myself* (UQP, 2025).

Yeena Kirkbright is a Wiradjuri poet, living and working on Darkinjung Country. She has been a participant in Sweatshop's All About Women of Colour emerging writers mentorship program, a runner-up in the Kuracca Prize for Australian Literature and Judith Wright Poetry Prize. Her work has appeared in several literary journals and anthologies.

Šime Knežević is a poet and playwright. His debut book-length collection, *In Your Dreams* (2025), was published by Giramondo. His chapbook *The Hostage* (2019) was a co-winner of the Subbed In Chapbook Prize. As a playwright, his recent works for the stage include *Various Characters* (2025) and *The Hen House* (2023).

Jennifer Kornberger is a poet, writer and artist based in Western Australia. Her practice spans publication, performance and installation works, and collaborations with artists in public art work. Her poetry has been commended in the Newcastle Poetry Prize and in 2016 she won the Tom Collins Prize. Her collections of poetry are: *I could be rain* (Sunline Press, 2007) and *The Twilight Observatory* (Five Islands Press, 2025).

Jo Langdon lives and writes on unceded Wadawurrung land. Her poetry collections are *Snowline* (Whitmore Press, 2012) and *Glass Life* (Five Islands Press, 2018). She has received fellowships from the Elizabeth Kostova Foundation, the National Library of Australia and the Wheeler Centre, and her fiction was a recent runner-up in the *Overland* Neilma Sidney Short Story Prize. Her recent writing also appears in journals including *Griffith Review, Island*, and *Meanjin*.

Bronwyn Lea is the author of *The Deep North* (George Braziller, NY), *The Other Way Out* (Giramondo) and *Flight Animals* (UQP). Her work has been widely anthologised and translated into multiple languages. She is Professor of Poetry and Creative Writing at The University of Queensland.

Xin Lee (李芯) is a Chinese-Malaysian writer and provisional psychologist based in Melbourne. She likes making things and making sense of grief and other intimate ways of being. Her works take shape in ceramic and poetic forms, which appear in *Island, Voiceworks*, and in warm personal correspondence.

Late Adelaide poet **Miriel Lenore** had a long and adventurous life: country kid in Victoria, botanist, researcher, traveller, student, activist, feminist, mother, grandmother. She spent twenty years in Fiji, forty years in the Australian women's movement and the Adelaide writing scene, ten years as a regular visitor to a Ngaanyatjarra community in the Western Desert. 'Bogong song' reflects Miriel's deeply feminist politics, wry wit and fascination with the naming of things. Miriel died in 2024 soon after her 96th birthday and before the publication of this poem in her ninth collection of poetry, *Driving to Mulberrygong.*

Bella Li is the author of *Argosy* (2017), *Lost Lake* (2018), and *Theory of Colours* (2021), published by Vagabond Press. Recent or forthcoming work can be found in *HEAT, Debris Magazine, Rabbit,* and *Runway Journal.*

Kate Lilley is a queer, Sydney-based poet-scholar. Her most recent poetry collection, *Tilt* (Vagabond Press), won the Victorian Premier's Prize. She was the co-editor of *BoAP 2024.*

Debbie Lim's poems have appeared regularly in the *Best Australian Poems* series and *Contemporary Asian Australian Poets,* among numerous other anthologies and journals. She received the 2022 Bruce Dawe National Poetry Prize and was shortlisted for the 2022 Peter Porter Poetry Prize. Her chapbook *Beastly Eye* was published by Vagabond Press. Her first full-length collection, *Bathypelagia,* was published by Cordite Books in 2025. She was born in Sydney, where she lives on Darramuragal land.

James Lucas was born in Sydney in 1965. He was educated at UNSW, where he won the University medal, and then completed a PhD in modernist poetry at Cambridge in 1997. His poems have appeared in Australian and international journals, and in the Henry Kendall Award, Newcastle Poetry Prize, Montreal International Poetry Prize, and Australian Catholic University Prize anthologies. His first volume *Rare Bird* (Recent Work Press, 2021) was short-listed for the Anne Elder Award. His second, *Jack Mundey in Red Square* (RWP), was published in 2025.

Shari Lynelle (also known as Shari Kocher) is an award-winning Australian poet who is also Deaf. She lives as a grateful guest on unceded Djaara Country in Central Victoria, Australia. Her most recent book, *Foxstruck & Other Collisions* (Puncher & Wattmann, 2021) was Highly Commended for the Kenneth Slessor Poetry Prize in the NSW Premier's Literary Awards (2022). www.sharilynelle.com

Shey Marque has published three collections of poetry. *The Hum Hearers* (UWAP, 2025), won the 2025 Wesley Michel Wright Prize, and was a finalist for the 2023 Dorothy Hewett Award. Her debut full collection, *Keeper of the Ritual* (UWAP, 2019) was a finalist for the Noel Rowe Award 2017. Her fourth collection, *Fugue State,* is forthcoming with 5 Islands Press.

Isabella G Mead's debut poetry collection, *The Infant Vine,* was published in 2024 by UWAP. Her work has also appeared in *Meanjin, Island, Griffith Review, Westerly, Cordite Poetry Review, Plumwood Mountain Journal* and *Anthropocene.* In 2024, she won the Venie Holmgren Environmental Poetry Prize. She lives, writes and raises her children on unceded Wurundjeri land.

Scott-Patrick Mitchell is a queer non-binary poet living on Whadjuk Noongar Country. They were the recipient of 2022's Red Room Poetry Fellowship, *Westerly*'s 2022 Mid-Career Fellowship and the 2023 winner of The XYZ Prize for Innovation in Spoken Word. Their debut poetry collection *Clean* (Upswell Publishing, 2022) was shortlisted for The Prime Minister's Literary Awards, The WA Premier's Book Awards, The Victorian Premier's Literary Awards and internationally in The Read Rainbow's Best LGBTIQA+ Books of 2022 Awards.

Jazz Money is a Wiradjuri poet and artist producing works that encompass installation, performance, film and print. Their writing and art has been presented, performed and published nationally and internationally. Jazz has written two award-winning poetry collections, *how to make a basket* (2021) and *mark the dawn* (2024), and the children's book *The Frog's First Song* (2025) illustrated by Jason Phu. Trained as a filmmaker, Jazz's first feature film *WINHANGANHA* (2023) was commissioned by the NFSA.

Marjon Mossammaparast is a poet from Melbourne. Her first collection of poetry, *That Sight* (Cordite Books), won the 2019 Mary Gilmore Award, was shortlisted for the 2019 Judith Wright Calanthe Award, and was commended in the 2018 Anne Elder Award. Her second volume, *And To Ecstasy*, was released in March 2022 through Upswell Publishing, and was shortlisted for the 2023 Kenneth Slessor Poetry Award. Her poems have been published widely in a range of Australian journals.

A melancholy figure on the lonely windswept streets of Newcastle, **David Musgrave** occasionally emerges from his habitual funk to write books of poems, of which *The Kool-Aid Dispenser* is his tenth. Often he claims to be wandering to and from the University of Newcastle, where he teaches creative writing. At other times he desultorily discharges his duties at the independent publishing house Puncher & Wattmann, which he founded in 2003. In his spare time he translates classical Chinese poetry and ferries his son around to his (Jingxi's, that is) many interesting extra-curricular activities, deriving further poems from his son's perceptive observations.

Omar Musa is an author, visual artist, rapper and poet from Queanbeyan. He has written two novels (including *Fierceland*), three books of poetry (including *Killernova*), five hip-hop records, and two plays—*Since Ali Died* and *The Offering (A Plastic Ocean Oratorio)*, with cellist Mariel Roberts Musa. His debut novel *Here Come the Dogs* was long-listed for the International Dublin Literary Award and Miles Franklin Award and he was named one of the *Sydney Morning Herald*'s Young Novelists of the Year in 2015. He has had several solo exhibitions, including his most recent, *All My Memories Are Mistranslations*.

S. Niroshini is an Australian writer and poet based in London. Her poetry pamphlet *Darling Girl* (Bad Betty Press, UK) was published in 2021. Three of her poems were included in the Bloodaxe anthology *Out of Sri Lanka: Tamil, Sinhala and English poetry from Sri Lanka and its Diasporas* (2023). Her writing has been published widely including *Poetry London*, *Cordite Poetry Review*, *Portside Review*, *Poetry Birmingham Literary Journal* and *The Georgia Review*.

Peter O'Mara lives in Hepburn Springs, Victoria. He has work published in magazines, journals, anthologies and online in Australia and overseas. These publications include *Angelaki, Cordite, Meanjin* and *Overland*. His work was included in *Best Australian Poetry 2008* (UQP). Peter published an art/TEXT manuscript, *How to do Words with Things* (treeElbow Publishing) with Patrick Jones (2008).

Thuy On was the Reviews and Literary Editor of *ArtsHub* for 4.5 years and also a former Books Editor of *The Big Issue*. She's an arts journalist, editor, critic and poet. Her three collections of poetry have been published by UWAP: *Turbulence* (2020), *Decadence* (2022) and *Essence* (2025).

Esther Ottaway is a Tasmanian/lutruwita poet, editor and mentor whose poetry has won or been shortlisted for many international and Australian prizes, including the Tom Collins, Woorilla, MPU International, Bridport, Montreal, and Mslexia. Her second book, *Intimate, Low-voiced, Delicate Things*, won both the $25,000 poetry prize and the People's Choice prize in the 2022 Tasmanian Literary Awards. Her new books are *She Doesn't Seem Autistic* and a landmark anthology of Australian disability writing, *Raging Grace* (co-edited with Andy Jackson and Kerri Shying).

Louise Oxley lives and writes in Lutruwita/Tasmania. Her poems have been widely published and awarded since the 1990s. She has won the Bruce Dawe, Melbourne Poets Union and Shoalhaven poetry prizes, among others. Her second collection, *Buoyancy*, was shortlisted in the WA Premier's Literary Awards. She has recently published her third collection, *Range Light*, with Walleah Press.

Luke Patterson is a Gamilaroi poet, folklorist and musician living on Gadigal lands. His debut poetry collection *A Savage Turn* is out now with Magabala Books. Luke's research and creative pursuits are grounded in extensive work with First Nations and other community-based organisations across Australia.

Charmaine Papertalk Green (1962–27 August 2025) was an Australian Indigenous poet, a proud Wajarri, Badimaya and Wilunyu woman of the Yamaji Nation. A visual artist, author, poet, storyteller and social science researcher, she shared her cultural knowledge in many different spheres. Charmaine had written five books, won several awards including the prestigious Australian Literary Society Gold Medal, and her poetry is studied as part of primary and school curriculum. Involved with the Yamaji Art Centre in Geraldton for over 22 years, she was their Chairperson. Charmaine was awarded the 2022 Magabala Fellowship 2022 and 2023 Red Room Poetry Fellowship and was a member of the national First Nation Aboriginal Writers Network.

Felicity Plunkett is a poet and critic living on Wangal land. Her books are *A Kinder Sea* (UQP), *Vanishing Point* (UQP) and *Seastrands* (Vagabond). She edited the anthology *Thirty Australian Poets* (UQP). She is *Australian Book Review*'s Poetry Editor.

Stephanie Powell is a poet based in Naarm/Melbourne. She is the winner of the AAALS Prize 2025, the Woorilla Prize 2024, the Ada Cambridge Prize for Poetry 2024 and has been previously shortlisted for the Woollahra Digital Literary Award (2024). She has three collections of poetry, *Bone* (Halas Press, 2021), *Gentle Creatures* (Vagabond Press, 2023) and *Invisible Wasp* (Liquid Amber Press, 2024). She lives and works on unceded Wurundjeri Woi-Wurrung land.

Mark Roberts is a writer, critic and publisher living on unceded Darug and Gundungurra land. He is the founder and co-editor of *Rochford Street Review* and *P76 Magazine*. Mark has published three books, the latest being *The Office of Literary Endeavours* (5 Islands Press) in May 2025. His work has been widely anthologised and has appeared in numerous magazines and journals in Australia and overseas.

Izzy Roberts-Orr is a poet and arts worker based on Wurundjeri Country in regional Victoria. Her debut poetry collection *Raw Salt* (Vagabond Press) won the 2024 Anne Elder Award.

Autumn Royal creates drama, poetry and criticism. Autumn was the founding editor of Liquid Architecture's *Disclaimer* journal and is interviews editor at *Cordite Poetry Review*. Her poetry collections include *She Woke and Rose*, *Liquidation* and *The Drama Student*, which was shortlisted for the 2023 Queensland Premier's Judith Wright Calanthe Award and the 2024 Prime Minister's Literary Award for Poetry.

Gig Ryan's *New and Selected Poems* (Giramondo, 2011); *Selected Poems* (Bloodaxe, 2012), was winner of the 2012 Grace Leven Prize for Poetry and the 2012 Kenneth Slessor Prize for Poetry. She has also written songs with Disband, *Six Goodbyes* (1988), Driving Past, *Real Estate* (1999) and *Travel* (2006). She was Poetry Editor of *The Age* 1998–2016, and received a PhD from Monash University (half creative writing, half research) in 2020, and is an irregular poetry reviewer, and is finalising her next book.

Micaela Sahhar is an Australian-Palestinian writer, academic and educator living on unceded Wurundjeri Country. Her essays, poetry and commentary have appeared in *Cordite, Meanjin, Overland, Rabbit, Southerly* and *Sydney Review of Books*, among others. She is a Wheeler Centre Next Chapter Fellow (2021), a grant recipient from the Neilma Sidney Literary Travel Fund (2022) and was commended for the Peter Blazey Fellowship (2024). *Find Me at the Jaffa Gate: an encyclopaedia of a Palestinian family* (NewSouth, 2025) is her first book.

Omar Sakr is a poet and writer born in Western Sydney to Lebanese and Turkish Muslim migrants. He is the acclaimed author of the novel *Son of Sin* and three poetry collections, including *The Lost Arabs*, which won the 2020 Prime Minister's Literary Award for Poetry. His collection, *Non-Essential Work*, was shortlisted for the Kenneth Slessor Prize and the ALS Gold Medal. His non-fiction work has been published widely, including in *The Guardian, The Sydney Morning Herald* and *SBS Life*. *The Nightmare Sequence*, a collaboration with Safdar Ahmed, is his latest work.

Sara M Saleh is a writer/poet of Palestinian, Egyptian, and Lebanese descent. Her debut novel, *Songs for the Dead and the Living* (Affirm, 2023), and her poetry collection, *The Flirtation of Girls* (UQP, 2023), have received multiple national and international prizes and shortlistings between them. Sara made history as the first poet to win both the 2021 Peter Porter Poetry Prize and the 2020 *Overland* Judith Wright Poetry Prize. Rooted in the belief that literacy is a tool for liberation, Sara has rallied communities of artists across continents to create generative, inclusive spaces for craft, connection, and critical consciousness.

Jaya Savige's most recent collection of poems, *Change Machine* (UQP 2020), was shortlisted for the Prime Minister's Literary Award, the Kenneth Slessor Prize and the Judith Wright Calanthe Award. His previous collections include *latecomers* (UQP 2005) and *Surface to Air* (UQP 2011). Born in Sydney, Jaya grew up on Bribie Island and in Brisbane. A former Gates Scholar at the University of Cambridge, he is poetry editor for *The Australian*, and currently lives in London with his wife and son.

Elfie Shiosaki is a Noongar and Yawuru writer. She is an Associate Professor at the College of Arts and Social Sciences at the Australian National University. Her research and teaching explores Indigenous desires for human rights and self-determination. She was the Editor of Indigenous Writing at *Westerly* from 2017 to 2021.

Ali Jane Smith is the author of the poetry collection *The Strange Matter* (Life Before Man 2025). She lives on Wodi Wodi Dharawhal Country.

David Stavanger is a poet and producer living on Wodi Wodi Dharawal land. He is the co-editor of *Solid Air: Australian & New Zealand Spoken Word* (UQP, 2019), *Admissions: Voices Within Mental Health* (Upswell, 2022), and is the author of *Case Notes*, which won the 2021 Victorian Premier's Prize for Poetry—his latest collection is *The Drop Off* (Upswell, 2025). David works as an Artistic Director at Red Room Poetry.

Saul Stavanger is an emerging filmmaker and writer living on Gadongal land, currently completing a Bachelor of Arts Screen: Production at AFTRS.

Svetlana Sterlin is the author of *If Movement Was a Language* (Vagabond Press), which won the 2023 Helen Anne Bell Poetry Bequest Award and was Commended in the 2024 Anne Elder Award. Based in Meanjin, Svetlana writes poetry, prose, and screenplays. Her work appears in *Australian Poetry, Cordite, Island, Westerly*, and elsewhere. A swimming coach and former swimmer, Svetlana is also the founding editor of *swim meet* lit mag.

Thom Sullivan is a writer, editor and reviewer of poetry. His debut book of poems, *Carte Blanche* (Vagabond Press, 2019), won the Noel Rowe Poetry Award and the 2020 Mary Gilmore Award. He grew up in Wistow/Bugle Ranges in the Mount Lofty Ranges, South Australia, and now lives in Adelaide, where he works in public policy.

Andrew Sutherland (he/they/she) is a Queer Poz (PLHIV) writer and performance-maker currently based on the unceded lands of the Kulin nation. He is the author of two collections of poetry, *Paradise (point of transmission)* and *Act Cute*, published in 2022 and 2025 with Fremantle Press.

Helen Swain lives in lutruwita on the foothills of kunanyi. She has worked in Multicultural Community Arts in Wollongong, taught high-school English and for many years taught EOL with migrants and refugees. As a spoken word improviser she has performed in Berlin, Paris and Australia. Writing poetry is a recent addiction and she now works as poet in residence in the public health sector. She has published three books of poetry including *Calibrating Home* with 5 Islands Press.

Dominic Symes lives quietly in Naarm. He writes poems, which over the last few years have appeared across Australian journals and anthologies. His debut collection *I saw the best memes of my generation* was highly commended in the 2024 NSW Premier's Literary Awards. In 2025, he was shortlisted for the *Overland* Judith Wright Poetry Prize in March and became a father for the first time in May. His second collection *Songs of love & hate speech* is forthcoming.

Lindsay Tuggle is a cross-genre writer. Her debut non-fiction book, *The Afterlives of Specimens*, was a cover feature in The New York Review of Books. Her poetry collection, *Calenture*, was one of *The Australian*'s Books of the Year and shortlisted for the Mary Gilmore and Anne Elder awards. Her work has been anthologized by both Oxford and Cambridge and featured in *Artist Profile, Commonplace, Cordite, Mascara* and *The North American Review*. Lindsay has been a Kluge Fellow at the Library of Congress, a Travelling Fellow with the Australian Academy of the Humanities, and a Writer-in-Residence at Bundanon Trust.

Lucy Van writes poetry and criticism. Her poetry collection, *The Open* (Cordite, 2021), was listed for the Stella Prize. With Anne Maxwell, her new book is *Australian Women's Historical Photography: Other Times, Other Views* (Anthem, 2024). Her forthcoming title is *MATERIAL* (Permanent Draft, 2025). She is an Honorary Fellow at the University of Melbourne, where she teaches literary studies.

Dženana Vucic is a Bosnian-Australian writer, editor and critic. Her essays and poetry have been published in *Australian Book Review, Australian Poetry Journal, Cordite, Kill Your Darlings, Meanjin, Overland, Sydney Review of Books*, and others. Her debut collection, *after war*, will be released by UQP in May 2026. She is Reviews Editor at *Cordite* and a Fiction Editor at *SAND*.

Corey Wakeling is a writer, scholar, and translator of modern and contemporary literature. He lives in Tokyo, where he teaches English literature as an associate professor at Aoyama Gakuin University. Author of four books of poetry, his most recent collection is *Uncle of Cats* (Cordite Books, 2025).

Connor Weightman grew up in Boorloo/Perth and currently dwells in Naarm/Melbourne. His debut poetry collection *Fivehundred Swimming Pools* was published by Rabbit Poetry in 2025.

Petra White is an Australian poet living outside London. She is the author of six poetry collections, most recently *That Galloping Horse* (Shearsman Books, 2024), which was a finalist in the Queensland Literary Awards and was shortlisted for the Prime Minister's Literary Awards.

Rachel White (she/her) writes on Kaurna land. Her poetry has been featured in *Kissing Dynamite*, placed highly commended in the 2022 Woorilla Poetry Prize, and was nominated for *Best Microfiction Anthology* and *Best of the Net 2024*. Her recent work appears in *Hawaii Pacific Review, The Shore, Thimble Lit, Lunch Ticket's Amuse Bouche*, and others.

Alison Whittaker is a Gomeroi writer and academic.

Panda Wong is a poet and editor living on unceded Wurundjeri land. She is one-half of music/poetry project lotus threads, with musician Hannah Wu. She is the author of *angel wings dumpster fire* and also released a collaborative poetry EP, *salmon cannon me into the abyss*, in 2022. She co-edited *Best of Australian Poems 2023*.

Grace Yee lives in Melbourne, on Wurundjeri land. She is the author of *Chinese Fish* (Giramondo), winner of the Victorian Prize for Literature, the Victorian Premier's Award for Poetry, and the Mary and Peter Biggs Award for Poetry at the Ockham New Zealand Book Awards. *Chinese Fish* will be published by Akoya (UK) in 2026. Her second book *Joss: A History* (Giramondo) was released in June 2025.

Xiaole Zhan (詹小乐) is a Chinese-Aotearoa writer and composer based in Naarm. Their work features in Auckland University Press's *New Poets 11*. They are also the recipient of a 2025 Creative New Zealand Fellowship, a 2025 Red Room Poetry Varuna Fellowship, the 2024 Kat Muscat Fellowship, and the winner of the 2023 *Kill Your Darlings* Non-Fiction Prize. Their name in Chinese means 'Little Happy', but can also be read as 'Little Music'.

Guest Editors

Nam Le is the author of three books, including *The Boat* and *On David Malouf.* His writing has been republished in modern classics series and is widely translated, anthologised and taught. Le's practice also encompasses criticism and screenwriting.

His most recent book *36 Ways of Writing a Vietnamese Poem* was published in March 2024 in Australia, the U.S. and the U.K. Poems from it have appeared in *Poetry, Paris Review, HEAT, Overland, American Poetry Review, Granta, BOMB, Yale Review, The Atlantic, Asymptote, Lana Turner* and elsewhere. The book was shortlisted for the Kenneth Slessor Prize, the ALS Gold Medal and the Mary Gilmore Award, selected as one of New York Public Library's Best New Poetry Books, and won the NSW Literary Award for Book of the Year.

Le's writing has also been recognised with honours including the PEN/Malamud Award, the Dylan Thomas Prize, the Anisfield-Wolf Book Award, the Melbourne Prize for Literature, and the Australian Prime Minister's Literary Award; and fellowships from the Fine Arts Work Center, the University of East Anglia, the Rockefeller Foundation, the Camargo Foundation, the Bogliasco Foundation, the Civitella Ranieri Foundation, and the Sidney Myer Foundation. He is a former fiction editor of the *Harvard Review.*

Jill Jones lives on unceded Kaurna land. Her latest book is *How To Emerge* (Vagabond Press, 2025). Her previous book, *Acrobat Music: New & Selected Poems* (2023), was short-listed for the 2024 John Bray Poetry Prize, long-listed for the 2024 ALS Gold Medal and commended in the 2023 Wesley Michel Wright Prize. In 2021 her book, *Wild Curious Air,* won the 2021 Wesley Michel Wright Prize, and in 2015 she won the Victorian Premier's Prize for Poetry for *The Beautiful Anxiety.* Her work has been widely published in most of the leading literary periodicals in Australia as well as in a number of print and online magazines in Canada, Czechia, Ireland, NZ, Singapore, Sweden, UK, and USA. Her poems have been translated into Chinese, Italian, Spanish, French, Czech and Dutch. An entry on her work is included in the current edition of *The Oxford Companion to Modern Poetry in English.* From 2008–2022, she was Senior Lecturer in the Department of English, Creative Writing and Film at the University of Adelaide, and is now a titleholder at the University. She currently works freelance and has previously worked as an arts administrator, film reviewer, journalist and book editor.

Acknowledgements & Publication Details

Adam Aitken's 'Cordon Sanitaire' appeared in *Australian Book Review*, April 2025.

Alice Allan's 'Craig fugue' was unpublished but written during the *BoAP 2025* timeframe. It subsequently appeared in *Overland 258*, September 2025.

Amanda Anastasi's 'Monostich X: Glimpses' appeared in the poet's collection, *Taking Apart the Bird Trap* (RWP, September 2024).

Chris Andrews' 'Queen Tide' appeared in *HEAT*, Series 3, Number 19, May 2025.

Alison J Barton's 'artificial bodies' appeared in *APJ 13.1, 'place, nonplace'*, August 2024.

Stuart Barnes' 'Pantoum' appeared in *Poetry Island Review*, Issue 144, September 2024 (ed. Jessica Traynor).

Judith Beveridge's 'The Stone' appeared in *Australian Book Review*, March 2025.

Kevin Brophy's 'An inventory of longing' appeared in the poet's collection, *An Inventory of Longing* (Whitmore Press, February 2025).

Lachlan Brown's 'Cut Common' appeared in *Moments: University of Canberra Vice-Chancellor's International Poetry Prize Anthology* (Centre for Creative and Cultural Research, December 2024).

Pam Brown's '2 stanzas from (*outer spacings*)' is an extract from the long poem '(outer spacings)' in *Endings & Spacings* (never-never books, 2021), published in *100 Poets* (Flying Islands Books, 2025).

Bonny Cassidy's 'A visitor' appeared in *APJ 14.1, 'walking'*, March, 2025.

Luoyang Chen's 'Twilight' appeared in *Westerly: Oceans*, November 2024.

Eileen Chong's '18 (from *We Speak of Flowers*)' is from the poet's collection, *We Speak of Flowers* (UQP, February 2025).

Emilie Collyer's 'trying to remember how it ends' appeared in *Marrow*, Issue 2, October 2024.

Amy Crutchfield's 'Grace Can Pour' was unpublished but written during the *BoAP 2025* timeframe. It subsequently appeared in *The Weekend Australian*, October 2024.

Madeleine Dale's 'Eleven Portraits of Drowning' appeared in the poet's collection, *Portraits of Drowning* (UQP, September 2024).

Natalie Damjanovich-Napoleon's 'Axe Marks in Tree Trunks' appeared in *Westerly 69.1*, August 2024.

Laurie Duggan's 'Rosebery Journal – October' appeared in *The Chalamet Review*, January 2025.

Anne Elvey's 'Stone Tongue' appeared in the poet's collection, *Intents* (Liquid Amber Press, April 2025).

Joel Ephraims's 'Upon the Passing of Tomas Tranströmer' appeared in the poet's collection, *Flying Car Kaleidoscope* (Vagabond Press, October 2024).

Michael Farrell's 'The Edit / An Edit' appeared in *Island Online*, August 2024.

Susan Fealy's 'Ricochet' appeared in *MENISCUS*, Volume 12, Issue 2, November 2024.

Toby Fitch's 'What Size is My Baby Poem' appeared in *Overland 256*, Spring 2025.

Holly Friedlander Liddicoat's 'desire #3' appeared in *APJ 13.2, 'desire'*, September, 2025.

Claire Gaskin's 'poverty' was unpublished but written during the *BoAP 2025* timeframe. It subsequently appeared in *Cordite: NO THEME*, August 2025.

Elena Gomez's 'The Hunted' appeared in *APJ 14.1, 'walking'*, March 2025.

Natalie Harkin's 'I see you I will never let you go' appeared in *APRON-SORROW / SOVEREIGN-TEA* (Wakefield Press, Adelaide, 2025).

Jennifer Harrison's 'After *Heimat*, a Film Series by Edgar Reitz, 1984' appeared in *Westerly 69.2*, April 2025.

Dominique Hecq's 'Otopos' appeared in *APA 11 2024*, Nov–Dec 2024.

Hasib Hourani's 'i see a photo of a great heron (extract from *rock flight*)' appeared in the poet's collection, *rock flight* (Giramondo, September 2024).

D.J. Huppatz's 'Icing' appeared in *Overland 70.2*, Winter 2024.

David Ishaya Osu's 'Birthplace' appeared in *Rabbit*, December 2024.

Holly Isemonger's 'Drinking Log: Day / Month / Year' appeared in *The Suburban Review 34 (Muscle)*.

Andy Jackson's 'Extinction song' appeared in *The Suburban Review 36 (Disability)*, December 2024.

Gurmeet Kaur's 'Flood Myth' appeared in *Rabbit*, December 2024.

Joel Keith's 'Trans Pastoral' was unpublished but written during the *BoAP 2025* timeframe. It subsequently appeared in *Overland 258*, September 2025.

Anna Kerdijk Nicholson's 'Dementia' appeared in *Island Online*, November 2024.

John Kinsella's 'Other Eminent Hands' appeared in *Australian Book Review*, July 2025.

Yeena Kirkbright's 'Work' appeared in *Overland 70.2*, Winter 2024.

Šime Knežević's 'Autofiction' appeared in the poet's collection, *In Your Dreams* (Giramondo, February 2025).

Jennifer Kornberger's 'The Creature Called Longing' appeared in the poet's collection, *The Twilight Observatory* (5 Islands Press, June 2025).

Jo Langdon's 'Epistolary' appeared in *Westerly 69.1*, August 2025.

Xin Lee (李芯)'s 'Chinese Funeral' appeared in *Island Online*, February 2025.

Miriel Lenore's 'Bogong song' appeared in the poet's posthumous collection, *Driving to Mulberrygong* (Wakefield Press, April 2025).

Bella Li's 'Le rêve de la rose' was commissioned for and first appeared in the concert program for *Silence & Rapture* (August 2024), by the Australian Chamber Orchestra.

Kate Lilley's 'Brink' appeared in *Overland*, Spring 2024.

Debbie Lim's 'Sister Cumulus' appeared in *HEAT*, Series 3 Number 18, March 2025.

James Lucas's 'Open the Frog App' appeared in the poet's collection, *Jack Mundey in Red Square* (RWP, May 2025).

Shari Lynelle's 'Poem approaching the possible' appeared in *APA 11 2024*, Nov–Dec 2024.

Shey Marque's 'Watching the Lightning Strike' appeared in the poet's collection, *The Hum Hearers* (UWAP, March 2025).

Isabella G Mead's 'The Scar' appeared in the poet's collection, *The Infant Vine* (UWAP, July 2024).

Scott-Patrick Mitchell's 'Apocalypse wears the ocean as if a dress' appeared in *Faith: 2024 ACU Prize for Poetry* chapbook (October 2024).

Jazz Money's 'out at night eatin' cars' appeared in the poet's collection, *mark the dawn* (UQP, July 2024).

Marjon Mossammaparast's 'January: Variations on Sadness' was unpublished but written during the BoAP 2025 timeframe. It subsequently appeared in *The Weekend Australian Review*, September 2025.

David Musgrave's 'Halfway Things' appeared in the poet's collection, *The Kool-Aid Dispenser* (RWP, March 2025).

S. Niroshini's 'Che Guevara Plants A Tree In Ceylon' appeared in Issue 12 of *Propel Magazine* (UK), ed. Tishani Doshi, July 2024.

Esther Ottaway's 'Night vision: apology to a late-diagnosed daughter *Autism*' appeared in *APA 11 2024*, Nov–Dec 2024.

Louise Oxley's 'Tenure' appeared in the poet's collection, *Range Light* (Walleah Press, June 2025).

Luke Patterson's 'Two Poems Shot on iPhone' appeared in *APJ 14.1, 'walking'*, March 2025.

Charmaine Papertalk Green's 'Jina Yanmanha – walking' appeared in *APJ 14.1, 'walking'*, March 2025.

Felicity Plunkett's 'Distance' appeared in *APJ 13.2, 'desire'*, September 2024.

Stephanie Powell's 'We are young and delicious' appeared in the poet's collection, *Invisible Wasp* (Liquid Amber Press, September 2024).

Mark Roberts' 'shadow birds' appeared in the poet's collection, *The Office of Literary Endeavours* (5 Islands Press, March 2025).

Autumn Royal's 'From mine to market' appeared in *Debris Magazine: Illuminated Manuscript*, October 2024.

Gig Ryan's 'Verification Factory' appeared in *Sick Leave Party Report III*, June 2025.

Micaela Sahhar's 'We are become' was unpublished but written during the *BoAP 2025* timeframe. It subsequently appeared in *Southerly*.

Omar Sakr's 'Holocaust in the genocide' appeared in *The Nightmare Sequence*, a collaboration with Safdar Ahmed (UQP, April 2025).

Jaya Savige's 'Spill' was unpublished but written during the BoAP 2025 timeframe. It will subsequently appear in *The Uncollected Animals: Poems for Our Nonhuman Kin* (Brooklyn, February 2026), ed. John Kinsella.

Elfie Shiosaki's 'Altered' appeared in the poet's collection, *Refugia* (Magabala Books, August 2024).

Ali Jane Smith's 'The Language of Flowers' appeared in the poet's collection, *The Strange Matter* (Life Before Man, March 2025).

David Stavanger's and **Saul Stavanger**'s 'Fifteen ways of being erased' appeared in the poetry collection, *The Drop Off* (Upswell, April 2025).

Svetlana Sterlin's 'If Movement Was a Language: Triptych' appeared in the poet's collection, *If Movement Was a Language* (Vagabond Press, October 2024).

Andrew Sutherland's 'We could have gone wandering out into the snow' appeared in *Westerly 69.1*, August 2024.

Helen Swain's 'Corpus mundi' appeared in the poet's collection, *Calibrating Home* (5 Islands Press, November 2024).

Dominic Symes's 'poem for nina' appeared in *Splinter*, Issue 1, November 2024.

Lindsay Tuggle's 'Sequela' was commissioned and published by *Artist Profile*, Issue 70, May 2025.

Lucy Van's 'Maybe If I Keep Having A Good Time All The Time All My Problems Will Just Go Away' appeared in *Sick Leave Party Report III*, June 2025.

Dženana Vucic's 'Because a wind blazes …' appeared in *Overland*, September 2024.

Corey Wakeling's 'More Albums by the Pixies' appeared in the poet's collection, *Uncle of Cats* (Cordite Books, January 2025).

Connor Weightman's 'Relative to the Body' appeared in the poet's collection, *Fivehundred Swimming Pools* (Rabbit Books, March 2025).

Rachel White's 'October 13th' appeared in *Hawaii Pacific Review*, December 2024.

Alison Whittaker's 'direct to ashfield' appeared in *APJ 13.2, 'desire'*, September 2024.

Panda Wong's 'some people read a poem' appeared in the *Cordite* online chapbook, *divine interventions*, May 2025.

Grace Yee's 'greener' appeared in the poet's collection, *Joss: A History* (Giramondo, June 2025).

Xiaole Zhan (詹小乐)'s '& whatever the man called each living creature, that was its name' was unpublished but written during the *BoAP 2025* timeframe. It subsequently appeared in *Starling*, Issue 20, August 2025.

www.ingramcontent.com/pod-product-compliance
Lightning Source LLC
Chambersburg PA
CBHW020600030726
47497CB00007B/2022